Duty

Alfred J. Lines

To MIKe
with many thanks.

Alfred J. Lines.

HISTORICAL CONTEXT

Leading figures are truly reported, notably:
The author
J.N. Mark, athlete and doctor
Headmaster of the Rev. David G. Loveday
The Rev. Major N. Crowhurst
Housemaster Charles B. Blackshaw
Peter S. Stirzaker
Ian G. Tait and brother J. A. Tait
Montague Aldridge
Mr. Wicks
The Rev. Cannon M.D. Sutton
The Rev. Cannon A.C. Phelps
Some others I have been unable to trace including D. Nichols, Nigel Ransom, A.J. Lyne, Faithful, and Beaumont

ACKNOWLEDGEMENTS

Editing by Catherine, Louise, and Mark Lines
Photographs by Mike Jeffreys Imaging, Shoreham-by-Sea

Dedicated to my family

CONTENTS

ALFRED J. LINES

FOREWORD

Dear Catherine,

I was prompted to write an account of some of my experiences at school by events in your life, which have some remarkable parallels and contrasts. Then, while engaged in it, and finding that the background of English school life was so different from the Canadian that you would have difficulty understanding it, the whole project expanded. During the process of writing and collating, I have, from time to time, read a few short pieces to friends and found that Canadian sensibilities are offended. Some parts are not fully explained at the first encounter, and are only understood by following the story through.

This is how it all happened and unfolded.

Some important points, e.g. the details surrounding the whistling episode, and the interview two weeks later became indelibly imprinted on my memory, so these are almost verbatim. But the various and often brief, conversations with Mark are written as condensations for greater clarity. Likewise there were several short encounters with Little A.J., and what is written is, rather, a summary. For there was much to discuss, and the friendship grew slowly.

Perhaps the theme that ties the stories together is the idea of duty. Some historical notes and the background of total war may help with the general context.

On 21st October 1805, off Cap Trafalgar, Nelson with twenty-seven ships of the line faced the combined French and Spanish Armada of thirty-three ships. At eleven fifty a.m., after an approach from windward that had taken the whole forenoon, the signal was hoisted on Nelson's flagship "Victory".

"England expects that every man will do his duty."

Only ten minutes later Admiral Collingwood in "Royal Sovereign" led the van into action, penetrating the enemy line. In fact the word "expects" was a second choice. Nelson had asked for "confides", but had given way to the signal crew's request on account of some flag difficulty. The original word would have reflected better the spirit of the fleet and the mood of the nation. The signal itself stands well in history, but almost certainly had no effect upon the conduct of the battle, which proved decisive.

Every English schoolboy becomes familiar with the painting of Nelson propped against a standing knee in the Orlop deck, pale and well aware that he was dying. On his way below decks he had said to his Captain:
"They have done for me, Hardy. My backbone is shot through."
Some of his last audible words were:
"Thank God! I have done my duty."

In the same way, in 1940 Churchill's historic address to the Commons and the people included the words:

"If we can stand up to him (Hitler) all Europe may be free and the life of the world may move forward into broad sunlit uplands. But if we fail, then the whole world including the United States, including all that we have known and loved, will sink into the abyss of a new Dark Age, made more sinister and perhaps more protracted by the lights of perverted science. Let us therefore brace" ('bace' – almost – he had difficulty with his r's) "ourselves to our duties, and so bear ourselves that, if the British Empire and its Commonwealth last for a thousand years men will say 'This was their finest hour'."

Some historians, especially in North America, have tried to make out that this speech was a turning point, or that it 'rallied the nation' from the brink of defeat. But this is nowhere near the truth. There was never, at any time, any consideration of the possibility of not defeating Germany. We were all fully braced up to the prospect of a long and hard war. There remained a lively interest in the Test (cricket at Lord's) that year. The leading hit song was "Maresy dotes and Dozy dotes…" (which I did not understand for years. You or Rachel could have explained it to me instantly.) No! We knew we had no friends or allies, and were all relieved when we found we did not have to carry the French any longer. We had forty – five million British, with eight million Canadian and six million Australians and New Zealanders to help, together with contingents from India, Nepal and Africa against the German population of eighty-three million who had been on a war footing for four years.

The King expressed it when solemnly informed of the Belgian capitulation:-

"Th-th-thank G-G-G-G—God!" He said, "That's our l-l-last B-B-B bloody Ally – s-s-s-surrendered."

History records that the C.I.G.S. had the same sentiments.

So, duty comes naturally to the English, and adversity is a stimulus.

One of the features which Mum will recognize is the extraordinary persistence of character, e.g.: in my own case – not quick to stand up for myself, usually fair-minded, but especially marred by my big mouth, and marked by arrogance. But magnanimity and sense of humour have served me well, and helped others, notably in the complex events of Lent

1944.

Most of this I have not told before to anyone. Many other stories remain in mind, but are probably not worth recording. The overall picture is a real reflection of life in any one of a few score of the great Boys' Schools as they were in the first half of the twentieth century and the latter part of the nineteenth. It is essential to understand that the public schools do little to mould the boys as they pass through, for by the age of entry each has his own character well formed: so that during the ensuing rapid growth through adolescence to manhood he begins to reveal and exploit his potential. In so doing he makes his mark upon the school. The nature and value of the school depend upon the calibre of the men who attend it.

The disciplinary system is not easily understood by North Americans, who are too often led to regard corporal punishment as immoral, despite the clear teachings of Moses and Jesus, the recorded experiences of Apostles, and many places in Proverbs. For us it was simple, seldom severe, and regarded as a necessary deterrent measure. A beating was always followed by a handshake, as if just punishment had in effect nullified the offence. There remained no grudge or ill will; no stigma. It was a bad event. But with youth's eternal optimism each of us thought it could only happen to someone else. Quite a surprise when it struck home! Many a time one heard: "I knew it would hurt like…. But I had just no idea it could be like that!"

At the time of writing the common teaching is that a person so punished necessarily suffers later from anger, depression, a poor self-image, pessimism, self-deprecation, under-achievement and various other conditions dreamed up under the D.S.M. system. We hear much, also of P.T.S.D. with the tale that for every U.S. soldier killed in Vietnam fighting, two suicides followed. Yet history does not record two million suicides after the American Civil War, or three million in England after WWI. And Mark Twain[1] who, after chastisement at school, having "had to grow a new hide every summer," later became a successful pilot and a famous author and public speaker, radiating the joy of living to many generations. These people had not been deluged with cocaine, hashish or psychiatric drugs. Neither had they fallen under the enervating, corrupting influence of Dr. Spock.

I can well imagine Samuel Clemens shrugging his shoulders and laughing with us as he says – "Psychiatry is bunk".

My own tale gives the lie (if it were needed) to the present common teaching – for my own experiences did not give rise to anger or ill will toward anyone who held and duly exercised authority. In contrast, some wonderful friendships grew, and my subsequent life story speaks for itself.

Likewise my father, birched at Cranbrook school, proceeded to academic brilliance, rowed at Henley, and became Director of Civil Engineering, Railway Board, India. i.e.: from the Hindoo Kush to Cape Cormorin and from the Brahma Putra to the Indus. (There was no Pakistan).

School was a microcosm, closely knit and in some ways monastic. Each of us knew his place in seniority. i.e.: in the continuum of upward progress. There was never a "them / us" situation. Promotion to prefect rank went especially to those who excelled at team sports. With higher rank came few benefits and much responsibility.

Individually we were vigorously healthy well-integrated young men, each in his own way looking forward to whatever the call of duty or the will of God might require. We were

---

[1] Mark Twain was a cognomen

always conscious of the war, and this enhanced our expectations of and care for each other. We were resilient in mind and body, each quietly confident that his fate was to excel in his chosen field.

We understood that we were privileged to be in a Public (i.e.: private) school and shared the awareness that boys from a state-school background would seldom join us, precisely because of the seemingly harsh discipline.

One other anecdote may shed some more light.

At a meeting of the Governing Board in 1997 it was revealed that some empty bottles, several beer and one sherry, had been found beneath floorboards of East House dormitory during the course of renovations. One of the Governors acknowledged these at once, and told the story.

"Mine!" He said.

He had been a day-boy, finishing his school career on a Wednesday afternoon. Boarders were to go home the following morning. He had arranged a celebration for the evening and brought the bottles.

But on the following day his housemaster, Charles B. Blackshaw, became aware of the deed, and administered justice with a cane and a strong right arm, although by this time the offender was no longer in statu pupillari, so quite outside his jurisdiction. The young man was apologetic to the Headmaster also, and the Rev. D.G. Loveday's gentle handwritten letter of understanding and acceptance is on record. No doubt there was good humour at the Board meeting, with other Old Cranleighans making the usual jests, "Well-deserved, I'm sure." "Hope it hurt!" etc. for justice done and amity preserved.

You have done well in life so far, in some ways against the odds, and after suffering for your faults, as I did. I trust that in working out the sequels from your own character you will have as much happiness as I have had and continue to enjoy. This is not a complete account of anything. But it may help you to understand some more about your Dad, and yourself by reflection and comparison.

1 BACKGROUND

In order to understand this account one must have some idea of English education as it was in the middle of the last century. There was a "state" school system with students together to the age of eleven when the best joined a grammar school, and others attended a less demanding school leading to an apprenticeship. In England, the leaving age was raised from fifteen to sixteen during the war, amid much debate and with good reason because the traditional age for starting apprenticeship was fifteen years. Sometimes a boy would start at sixteen. But in this, strictly class-arranged system, the artisans were jealous of their position and anyone who had failed to enter apprenticeship before his seventeenth birthday was thereafter prevented from entering any trade. He was to be a labourer without any possibility of acquiring journeyman status. An apprenticeship was standardized to five years long and the wages during that period were, for the first two years, pitifully low; and still by the fifth year low enough to compel the apprentice to remain at home. Only when he had achieved his journeyman status, passed his trade test and had papers in hand, could he expect a wage that would enable him to live an independent life. All this has been vigorously entrenched by the trade unions, so that the class society seemed to be not a thing imposed by any upper stratum but one rooted in the English character and maintained with great enthusiasm by artisans. Another feature was that once a man had a trade, then in time of war, he might enter another, but only on condition that afterward he return to his original one; and during the time when he is doing this second trade, he is not allowed to earn the full wage, even though the difference is only one or two percent of the official journeyman's rate.

Those conventions served well in those days when conditions were not changing rapidly and manufacturing was labour intensive. Now that it is capital intensive requiring high skills and, at a lower level, very little education, there is no middle ground. The old crafts are disappearing. For instance, a man who has served his time as a brass founder has a very little chance of lucrative work in the present day. During the first half of the twentieth century and the latter part of the nineteenth trades were much more fixed and a man who had apprenticed as a riveter could expect to remain in the same work for the whole of his life and would expect his sons to enter similar trades without any risk of having the whole industry disappear - the kind of calamity that happened on Clyde-side where twenty miles of ship yards vanished during three decades.

In parallel with State education was the so-called public school system, truly public because it was open to anyone who could pay to enter or could win a scholarship. The first two public schools, Eton and Harrow, are known worldwide and are fairly ancient. In the middle of the nineteenth century there was a great boom in the development of schools. This was led by men like Dr. Arnold of Rugby. Many were built to meet the demands of the merchants of the middle class. This led to some specialization. Most of these schools are based on Anglican faith and have ordained ministers as Headmasters and senior teachers. Most also have several ex-service men on their staff. A few are entirely Roman Catholic. There is at least one good evangelical public school in the West Country; Christ's Hospital is distinguished by its habit that is something like that of a monk, not from a long tradition but as innovation from the mid-nineteenth century.

These schools have served England well for years for many purposes. They provide a good source of ordained ministers of the established church. The Evangelical public school in the West Country produces many splendid Christians and has supplied a steady stream of missionaries to field service overseas. Another was founded by the East India

Company to prepare young men for administrative duties in India. But one of the leading features is the military training aspect. Most have a Corps which used to be called OTC (Officers Training Corps) and during the war became changed to Junior Training Corps. Training is simply like boot camp. For at least one afternoon or sometimes a whole day per week the boys change into army or air force uniform and become cadets, undergoing squad drill, arms drill, weapons training, and unarmed combat. There are proficiency tests.

A good idea of a typical public school can be obtained by reading Rudyard Kipling's book, Stalkey and Co., which is partly autobiographical. Churchill's story of his early life includes some vivid descriptions of life at Harrow.

Entry to a public school happens at the age of thirteen. In peace time, boys leave at the age of eighteen, sometimes nineteen, usually to go to University, but often into the services where they compete for officer status. Prior to entry to a public school it is usually necessary to go to a preparatory school. These "Prep" schools are smaller institutions, containing forty to one hundred boys, and provide introduction to a disciplined life. There is almost no spare time that is not closely supervised. The best of these prep schools provide high standards of learning, so that although the public schools are open to entry from any walk of life, in fact the prep schools make themselves expert at enabling boys to do well in the scholarship competitions.

The financing of public schools is interesting. Some such as Christ's Hospital have large benefactions or tracts of land. Some are increasing their ownership of land in order to keep their independence and make it much less likely for State takeover to happen. However, the threat of nationalization has been a growing concern of many. Eton, for instance, is reputed to have plans well prepared for re-founding in the

Irish Free State if socialism should threaten to change the character of their school in England.

One of the most recent innovations has been the introduction of girls. This would have been unheard of, almost unthinkable in the middle of the twentieth century. By the end, it was accepted and of course, the influence of the girls is in most ways excellent because it improves the academic standing, helping boys to compete more gently and fairly with one another. It also tempers the language which was sometimes quite appalling. So the introduction of the co-ed feature contributes to the sense of fairness which will now be even more obvious as part of the English character.

Now to the personal side of this story.

In my early life, I was plagued by some sicknesses with what seems to have been rheumatic fever, though I was never told that at the time. I remember being kept in one room for well over a year, having my temperature taken twice a day, never feeling quite well. And I remember the wonderful thrill I felt when I had a normal temperature for both morning and evening readings; but the situation soon changed and I was back to low grade fever all the time. I don't remember joint pains, but was continually being told that I had a weak heart. I suppose this meant that I had a murmur of some kind.

Finally, boarding school began to happen, and I was sent to a small school in the middle of East Anglia, which catered for about ten boarders. The rest were day pupils. Only two of the boarders were boys. One of the leading characteristics of this school, run by two Canadians, who were not French themselves, was that French was the only language spoken at some meals every week, or we were talking French all day or for a whole week at a time. However, we never learned to write any French; it was entirely oral teaching. I also remember, because I kept having to stay at home slightly sick instead of going to school, that when I had been at home, usually taking an arithmetic book with me, I would return to school saying that I had done such and such an exercise and would skip it and go to the next. Then I would turn over the page and do the next exercise and I would quickly look at the thing and see that it was quite easy and say, "Oh I did that too." So, I missed out an enormous amount of the arithmetic book and worked through it quickly and quite easily. By subterfuge, I more than made up for having missed a good deal of school time.

At the age of ten and a half, it was realized that I would have to go to a genuine prep school and I was put into Tormore, a boarding school in East Kent. Kent is a fairly cold place on the South East coast of England and is blasted with an East wind often in winter. Deal used to be an important passenger take off point for the new world. (John Wesley left from there and returned to Deal, before he was converted, long before his evangelical campaigns started in the eighteenth century.) This was because of its situation. It is at the North-Eastern end of the English Channel and the prevailing wind is South-West so that sailing ships, travelling through The Downs, a narrow area between the Goodwin Sands and the East Kent Coast, have difficulty beating against the wind and getting out of the Channel to start their voyage overseas. Consequently, at any time, there would be many sailing ships anchored in The Downs waiting for favorable wind. Then the fore-and-aft rigged small ships could start quickly and later the square riggers would brace their yards up and make sail to head down the Channel.

During the early part of the war in 1939 and early 1940, merchant ships were held up at anchor, being inspected for contraband by the British navy before they were allowed through to the low countries or Scandinavia and the Baltic states. This was a wonderful field for German aircraft and U-boats and a good place for magnetic mines. Every Sunday our school would walk down to the sea front, then about a mile along it and back to Upper Deal. We used to count the wrecks every week. The maximum number was reached just before the school was evacuated (the Germans began to install their heavy guns on the far side of the Channel). At that time we could count the masts, funnels and upper works of no less than forty-two ships sunk on the Goodwin Sands and in the Downs.

Our school was not an old one. It had been taken over by the current Headmaster who was a former army officer from the First World War. He had been wounded at the Gallipoli landings in the Dardanelles campaign of 1915. The mathematics teacher, who also taught Latin and History, was an older man, too old for the First World War, but was a splendid teacher and always made history lessons fascinating for us. He could even make Latin quite interesting. This school, Tormore, had a unique system whereby there were forms one, two, three, four, five, lower sixth and upper sixth, but separate maths classes in reverse order from sixth up to one at the top. Promotion from one form to another could be obtained at the end of any term and promotion in the maths classes was quite independent of other work. At the time, the best subjects to learn to win a scholarship into a public school were Latin and Greek. By the age of thirteen, the clever boys had spent two years in the upper sixth form in the prep school and were good at Latin, able to write Latin verse, also good at Greek and translating Greek New Testament. However, I had a late start and at the age of ten and a half was put into the third form where I found that the average age of the boys was nine years! So, I had to work hard to catch up and managed to spend about a year in the sixth form but was not good enough to learn any Greek or Latin verse composition. However, I have always enjoyed science, and was able to turn that interest to my advantage in the Cranleigh Scholarship competitions, when the life-cycle of the mosquito was asked.

I was prevented from vigorous activity in school sports and not encouraged in games at all. Sports were an important part of school life. The Headmaster was good at soccer and cricket.

I had a distinct advantage in French in that I didn't have to learn grammar. When we were writing French I found that I could usually do the sentences right by the sound. Then the time came for a scholarship at Cranleigh. I did this with some confidence in the French oral and music including singing and piano. I did not find out until I was about to leave Cranleigh school that I had earned the highest aggregate mark; but since I was weak in classics, I was awarded the third scholarship.

Cranleigh had been founded in the middle of the nineteenth century, and greatly expanded with new buildings in the early 1930's. The new building was steel, whereas the old was largely wood and brick. The Headmaster was an ordained minister of the church and a brilliant Greek and Latin scholar. He would walk into his Greek Testament classes without a copy of the Greek text. He didn't need this because he knew it by heart in Greek. It was a hobby to translate the leading article of the Times into Latin. The second master had been a trench Parson in the First War. The commander of the Corps (the Junior Training Corp), Major Westwood used to be known as "Woof Bang". Our East Housemaster was Lt. Blackshaw, a caricature of an army officer. He was a survivor from trench warfare including the Somme, making him a rare kind of person because so many officers had been killed in that campaign.

Cranleigh was my introduction to really tight discipline. The school day started with rising at seven o'clock, when a bell went. Breakfast was at half past seven, and the whole school trooped down to the dining hall on the ring of the bell; but not into it. We simply stood outside, waiting for the school prefect for the week to open the door. This done, he would say: "Right! Go in." Then we could walk in talking and stand by our appointed places, until suddenly there was a sharp knock with a gavel from head table. Then at once every boy stood at ease, facing the front behind the bench. The Grace was said. When we heard head table sitting down, we could sit also, and start to eat and talk. At the end of the meal there was another "knock up" with the gavel and at once all conversation ceased. Every boy had his hands behind his back, sitting stock still, facing the front. When we heard head table rise we would do the same, stand behind the bench at ease waiting for the final Grace to be said, and for the head table to walk out of the dining hall. That accomplished, the school prefect for the week would turn and say: "Speak". Then conversation could begin again. We could continue the meal or walk out, if we had finished it, in our own time.

Regulations governed our attendance at each class. Each teacher had his own room. Boys would move from one to another at change of periods carrying the necessary books. Talking in the corridors was officially forbidden but of course took place. At lunch time and again at evening meal, the routines were repeated.

Sports were important at any time. During the war, we were restricted to sporting activities on four days per week, because of the tight rationing. The caloric intake went down to two thousand per day. So, on four days a week we would have maybe a rugby practice, a short cross country run, or a rugger game. But in addition to these four events each week, on three mornings we also had physical training which was done as a drill, the houses breaking up into their individual squads. Each was taken by one of the house prefects. There was one squad for the elder boys who could run faster, and one for younger ones and the new boys. During the later part of the war the physical training periods became entirely devoted to unarmed combat, obstacle courses and what would be regarded now as the martial arts. We were all imbued with the longing to get into the war and start to kill Germans ourselves.

One of the results of all this vigorous exercise was that the school of more than three hundred boys was a collection of very fit young people. Now, if they are all of one gender and they are in their early and middle teen years, there is a danger of homosexual activity. Consequently, it was essential that in the school there was no possibility for privacy at any time from the beginning of term to the end. This was something of a shock when one found that, for instance, all toilets were in rows facing each other with no doors. There was a small swimming pool but entirely inadequate and without a proper water circulation system so that it was always cold; and later in the summer time when it began to warm up it also began to get too dirty and had to be closed. Swimming was supervised. Everybody knew how to swim. Bathing trunks were forbidden; we swam naked.

Once a week, Friday afternoon, the whole school changed into uniform. In 1940, we wore Field Service Dress. This included putties and knee length breeches. These might have been good for the older soldiers who probably had varicose vein troubles serving in the tropics with long distance marching to do. F.S.D. was replaced by the much simpler battle dress. We had to give careful attention to polishing boots and buttons. We hated doing this as brass tarnished so easily.

When we had to "fall in" on the parade ground there were six or seven platoons separating for various drills. Squad drill was the first. This seemed to go on week after week until we became slick and perfect at it; then arms drill. We had the Lee-Enfield Mark Four rifles, until these were taken and we had to drill with captured Italian ones which we despised.

Then weapons training, more unarmed combat and various other details like Morse (this was more important in the air training corps) and signaling routines. This proved an immense advantage when it came to time of war and we had to compete on equal ground with the called up men who were not keen to serve. We knew the right language. We knew how to obey an order immediately. At drill the public school boys were outstanding. We knew how to lead the squad, and were usually much fitter than the average grammar school boy. This led to rapid promotion amongst the public school men. Almost none were conscripted, because even though some went for deferred service with scientific qualifications and started engineering or medical work, most of us preferred the active armed forces. We went to things like tank corps, paratroops, Fleet Air Arm, submarines, and fighter pilots; the places where all the action was and, of course, rapid promotion. It seemed that death only happened to the other guy and we were not much disturbed when we had reports of so and so. "Oh yes, he wiped himself over the airfield in training", or "Do you remember Calvert? What a shame! He got home all right, but then he took off again to land at his own airfield, and burned up at the end of the runway. Pity really! Nice guy!" The whole of the South of England was involved in the war. There were sixty thousand civilians killed in air raids – about the same number of dead as Canada had in the armed forces on all fronts.

Commanding the parade was always "Major Woof Bang". Lieutenant Blackshaw was there sometimes. There was a Sergeant Major present at every parade and he turned up even when we were in Mufti on weekdays and would sometimes see us "slouching" as he called it. We would hear his stentorian voice from an enormous distance; "Pick it up there! Get in step, left, right, left, right!" He was really in character when a Heinkel appeared. This was shortly after Whitgift School had been bombed. He immediately took a Browning out of the armoury and was trying to take pot shots as it went round the village. It did not make a serious attack at the school, just flew away -much to his disappointment!

In this atmosphere of war, and the camaraderie involved, friendships were easy to make and stood firm. One of my friends was Peter Stirzaker who was, in fact, a fine athlete. He was an admirer of Hackenschmidt who had been a wrestler and a body builder long before the days of Charles Atlas or Ben Wieder. Stirzaker himself was a sprinter and good at rugger and all the rapid sports, but did not have such a good eye for a ball as the cricketers. We were in the fifth form together (five B) when I first went there. But he held himself back to do more maths because he intended to go to a technical school rather than a University, to study marine engineering. I was at that time thinking of naval architecture.

We confirmed our friendship after the news of the Denmark Straight naval action. The school, in fact the whole country, was dismayed by the loss of Hood. Stirzaker and I knew at once why it had happened. She had a thin armoured deck, like the battle cruisers at Jutland where three ships had blown up for the same reason in 1916. Admiral Beatty made the timeless remark "Something's wrong with our bloody ships today. Turn two points to the northward", in other words, "engage the enemy more closely". Hood had indeed blown up, exactly as we expected, having had her armoured deck pierced so easily. We both knew the details of her tonnage, horsepower on each shaft, her main armament of eight fifteen-inch guns, like Bismarck, and her secondary armament of twelve five point five inch guns commandeered after having been manufactured for the Greeks. They were the only five point five inch guns in the fleet and were in fact obsolete. Hood had been completed in 1922 at the cost of one hundred pounds a ton. Contrast, for instance, the German "Pocket Battleships" at three hundred and seventy five pounds per ton (£375/ton) – five years later. So Hood was old, cheap, wet in a seaway, and long overdue for refit;

yet still the most beautiful capital ship ever built. She had been reinforced with external torpedo bulges and a greater draft with very little change in speed because all the extra displacement was below the water line which left her unchanged in beam – sleek as ever. She could achieve thirty-one knots. But she had this fatal defect – a thin armoured deck. We had known that her only hope against Bismarck would have been to close the range as quickly as possible. In this she failed.

So, Peter Stirzaker and I had much in engineering interest in common. But he had most of his friends among the sporting fraternity, so that he achieved rapid promotion and became our House Captain. Peter and John Mark were on the school Rugger Fifteen; while Peter was captain of our house rugger team and a house prefect and then House Captain following this. John Mark became Senior Prefect for the school as he was the captain of the First Fifteen. This was the usual arrangement.

After breakfast each day, there was an interval in which we could complete homework or do any other detail like polishing shoes, and finally Chapel Line was marked by a bell at ten minutes to nine o'clock. By this time, every boy had to be in place in order of seniority, in his houseroom. House prefects carried out a brief inspection of dress, tidy hair, polished shoes and so on. Then by houses, we walked to the Chapel (or marched) one behind another, and those in the choir took off from the general file and into the choir stalls. Music was done well. We always had a good choir director. On arrival, I was a soprano. Later as my voice began to break, I was singing alto parts and later bass or tenor. Every morning there was a bidding prayer followed by one of the Psalms appointed for the day. We had to open the Psalter and the chant book separately and read from both at the same time. It gave us good practice at sight reading. The sound was beautiful. There was a reading by one of the prefects or a school master. Following that a hymn, when once again we read music written, from the Ancient and Modern, or from the Public School Hymn Book. Then the school walked out once again in house order and directly to the first class, Divinity, which lasted form after Chapel, about nine fifteen, until nine forty-five. There was a break in midmorning and classes finished at ten to one for lunch at one o'clock.

In the afternoon, on three days each week, there were two class periods, each of forty-five minutes, followed by tea and a bun, after which we could change for games immediately. Supper was at fifteen minutes to seven. On the other three weekdays, we had no afternoon classes. Since the mid-day lunch was a heavy meal, we were not allowed to change for games until two o'clock. At four fifteen was "Call over", a simple roll call in each houseroom.

For any new boy, introduction to this routine was difficult. In East House, a junior of about one year's standing was assigned to look after each new arrival. Holden introduced himself to me, and lost no time explaining routines and requirements. He took some care to elaborate on the discipline aspect, as this was perplexing at first, and to some was forbidding.

"It's like the Army in some ways," he said, "but much worse in others. You will be wise to ask no questions, or at least if you have any, come to me first. Never question an order from a prefect – you know them because they wear their coats open, unbuttoned. A school prefect is allowed to wear a blazer. Always stand aside for a school prefect. When one comes into the houseroom, stand up and shut up till he leaves or says, "Speak". If you are nearest to the door when he walks towards it, open it for him.

You are bound to have a few surprises with a stick. Don't worry about it. It's usually a Corporal's cane, like in prep schools. But, be warned, the school's prefect's standing order: "Each stroke shall be laid on with all possible force." In addition, you will find that these guys are all better at it than any prep school Headmaster. Standard is six. And do remember – You don't make a sound or move an inch. The lower class boys, "(not a reference to academic standing, but a recognition of class distinction in which public school boys and men expected higher standards from themselves and each other)" – oh yes – there are always a few here – they usually squeal. We don't. O.K.? Another thing, we always shake hands afterwards. Usually doesn't bleed. Might ooze a bit – sticks to your pants. But it's all gone in three weeks – unless it's the old four-foot. But that's not used much now."

I was to have my first such surprise not many weeks later. One evening when the bell was rung at eight twenty-five to start the five minute break during "prep"; I went to retrieve one of my text books from a boy to whom I had lent it. He was bigger and stronger than I (most boys were) and in the struggle that ensued I was doing badly, but not giving up, when Calvert, a school-prefect-at-large (i.e.: junior to our House Captain) came into the houseroom. We had not noticed his entry, and continued to wrestle over the book until he ordered loudly:

"Stop fighting," and seized the book. He turned towards the table where Bull, the house prefect on duty for the week had been sitting (he was now standing) supervising prep, and handed my textbook to him. I immediately said:

"Hey! That's my book, and I need it now."

Calvert turned to me and said, quietly:

"You're both on the list tonight for taking no notice when I came in, and you Lines, should know better than to speak to me like that. I'll see you in the bathroom in two minutes."

He turned to Bull:

"Lines will be late for the eight thirty bell. Put them both on your list for six tonight."

I reached the bathroom before Calvert, as he had to fetch a stick from his study at the opposite end of the school building. He came back, after running the stairs both ways, saying:
"So, I'm just nicely warmed up. You get four, because I'm doing it. Normally it would be six, no question – just so that you understand there is nothing personal in this, O.K.?"

I found myself saying:

"Oh yes, I see, and thanks, really."

I remembered Holden's advice, and followed it. Then the sincere handshake seemed to put it all away neatly. As we left, Calvert was explaining why the bathrooms were always used for this procedure:

"For one thing, there's plenty of space, and that's certainly needed when it's one of the longer canes. For another, if you have to vomit or start to faint- what better place? Not many people do either.

That's the first time for you isn't it? The bruises last two weeks or more, but you had better remember it longer than that. I think you will. Bull is going to remind you at half past nine tonight as well. You should be all right. You've had that before anyway." Calvert was cheerfully expressing his confidence in me – that I would not crack. And, as he expected, when two boys were slippered in the dormitory at 9:30, neither of these gave any evidence of having had four strokes with a cane just one hour before-hand, though it was common knowledge. That was my introduction to the system. It was effective, simple, without guile and remarkably hygienic.

Since I was two to three years younger than most of the boys in form five B, I was slow to make any close friendships. I was repeatedly surprised and disappointed by the short attention span and seemingly low intelligence of most of those around me. Then, as now, I did not suffer fools gladly. Peter Stirzaker was an exception.

The same difficulty was found by scholars in other houses. Some schools have tried to address the problem by grouping scholars in one house. Westminster used to do this. Whatever system is followed, the few who are capable of rapid academic progress find that they are often isolated from, and excluded by a majority of their peers, so that they stream themselves into an elite, and can, in turn, benefit by the loss of social influences which might otherwise hold them back.

Although my first impression was that the emphasis on sports achievement as the sole basis for advance to prefect status was ill conceived, I had to concede later that the quality of leadership so evoked was perfectly suited to the needs of war. Peacetime would impose different standards, so that the evolving public schools could still provide the leaders for the new meritocracy.

Academic progress was monitored, as in Churchill's Harrow fifty years before, by "lists" every two to three weeks. At this ritual, the whole school was assembled in the speech hall. The Headmaster, from the stage, read out the grade awarded to each boy for the previous fortnight's work, starting with the lowest form, three C. The A names were read out first, usually few, followed by some slow handclaps, The B's were the most numerous, heard in silence. Then the few C's, followed by some low hisses or gentle rumbling of feet. Finally the D names, if any, after which the Head would say:

"The D's will leave now."

So they did, reporting immediately to the Second Master, The Reverend Major Crowhurst, to be caned.

This was repeated with every form, finishing with his own group six A, classics. In fact, there were few D's, and lists held no terror for most of us.

I had one close call. My attitude to French was frankly lazy. There were many reasons for this. One was my clear advantage in the oral, and this went with a hearty contempt for the teacher's accent. Lt. Charles Blackshaw taught French, and either could not or would not pronounce the "R" sounds correctly. Another reason was that I came to his class with a better vocabulary than most boys, and often found nothing new in the daily learning requirement of ten words. I did not realize that I was falling far behind in grammar.

One day, shortly before lists we had a vocabulary test. At the beginning of the class Blackshaw announced:

"Lines has two C's marked for grammar. A third C will provide a "D" in French. A "D" in one subject means a "D" for the list, and a "D" for the list provides? You know what follows, Lines. So we'll start with the vocab test, covering all the words you've learned this last fortnight. Two rounds."

I was instantly frightened, which was exactly what he wanted. He started asking us a word each, going round the whole form. At my turn, a pause, then:

"Lines! How do you say, 'It's raining cats and dogs?' I warn you it is not 'chats et chiens'."

I knew this, but could not resist waiting for some seconds

while he drummed his knuckles on the desk.

"Il pleut a verse." I said quite solemnly.

Blackshaw whistled: "Phew! I have one more chance, haven't I, Lines?"

Later, someone didn't know what a swallow was. Nor did the next boy, nor the next. Blackshaw sat back.

"Anyone – a swallow?" he asked.

My hand went up. He looked at me.

"Une hirondelle. Vraiment vous en avez plusieurs chez vous maintenant, n'est ce pas?"

I was careful to sound all the R's correctly. He smiled and nodded agreement. There were many nests under the eaves of his house.

"And I still have one more chance, haven't I, Lines?"

Next time it was my turn, he asked:

"What is a statesman?"

"Un homme d'etat."

He raised his eyebrows and acknowledged:

"A for the test, B for French."

After class, someone asked:

"Lines, was that innate genius or just the luck of Old Nick?"

"Genius, of course," I was quick to answer.

"On m'a demandé les deux mots les plus difficiles du matin, mais j'ai eu raison parfaitement avec tous les duex – et tous les autres – par exemple les votres étaient très faciles, n'est ce pas?"

"Shut up! Bloody Frenchman!" I was often bratty with these older boys, and they would not have known how bad my French was. But this was no joke. One of the older boys clouted my head with a book. This was 1941 and we all hated and even despised the French. They had negotiated their own surrender to an inferior German force, leaving most of their enormous army in the South of France, remote from the scene of action. Then, while the British Right flank in the North was left to the French they collapsed, as did the Belgians on the left, so being called a Frenchman was almost as frightening as the prospect of a D in the lists.

Blackshaw's classes were often light hearted. One of the papers in the School Certificate exam was a free composition, for which the appointed invigilator read a short story in French and left us to rewrite it in our own words. In one class Charles laboured the point that any examiner faced with a pile of papers all beginning with the words: "Il y avait une fois" might be tempted to express his feelings in ways unwelcome to the candidates.

"Use any form of words,' pleaded Charles, "other than, 'Il y avait une fois'."

Came the day of the exam, with sixty boys at desks in the Speech Hall, facing centre stage awaiting an invigilator. To our surprise, Blackshaw was that person. He made a ceremony of opening the envelope on stage and removing the printed story, which he would have to read to us.

As he looked at the first page, he frowned, then opened his eyes widely, puffed out his cheeks and banged the page down on the desk. Then for a second or two, turned his back, turned round again and made as if both hands were shaking. He took up the paper and opened his mouth as if to speak. Then stopped and finally looked at us all and back at the paper. He read the printed words:

"Il y avait une fois…"

Roars of laughter and stamping of feet greeted him. But the tension was broken, and he was free to read the whole story, for us to reproduce in our attempts at French prose.

The French oral exam I enjoyed. Two examiners asked me to explain how a sash window worked. In the evening, after prayers in the dormitory, Charles was congratulating me on being top of the French oral: "With distinction and éclat," But again I did badly in grammar and was not awarded a distinction in French, merely a credit.

2 THE EVENT – DURING LENT TERM, 1944

There was one schoolmaster, older than many of the others, who was not in charge of a house and had been introduced to the school late in the war, Mr. Wicks. He had perpetual difficulty controlling his classes and the third and middle forms took advantage of this. He had the unfortunate habit of whistling his "s" sounds quite loudly. At one evening meal, when he gave the first grace, which was, "May the Lord bless what His bounty has provided", each "S" was distinctly whistled. Of course we began to grin and titter a little. Then we forgot it 'til the end of the meal. However, the second grace, after the meal, was always, "For these, and all His mercies, may God's holy name be praised," and once again the whistling, this time more pronounced, had us all giggling. We found it difficult to keep still. Many of us were whistling – hissing between our teeth. Of course, this can't be seen; one can do it without any change of expression. (A change of facial expression was sometimes punishable. There was in fact a rule against "bearing a facial expression prejudicial to the maintenance of good order and discipline". Many a time a prefect or the Sergeant Major would shout at a boy in a squad, "What's that smile doing on your face? Take it off!" So we were careful about facial expressions. To break even this rule would show disrespect for authority.)

On this occasion, after high table had finished walking out, the Senior Prefect, instead of turning as usual and saying "Speak", shut the door behind him and then said loudly:

"Will all those who whistled, report to One North bathroom at seven-thirty".

Now, there was one reason for reporting to One North

bathroom at seven-thirty. It was always sinister. The disposition of the houses was that on the first floor up from the ground there were three houserooms on the South side of the corridor, Two and Three South, One North, and One and Four South. One North bathroom was on the North side, immediately opposite their houseroom. Each houseroom would contain fifty to sixty boys doing their preparation, starting on the sound of the bell at seven-thirty. In the ten or twenty minutes remaining between the Senior Prefect opening the door before allowing us out and my appointment time at seven-thirty at One North bathroom, I was able to get books out for prep in my study on the top floor. I knew that I would be late starting prep that night. Then I made my way towards One North bathroom and found a crowd of boys walking rather hurriedly in the opposite direction; some tried to turn me round saying: "Come on! We're not staying". However, I had an appointment at a certain time at a certain place and what was to be done but to obey an order?

As I arrived at One North bathroom, not a soul in sight! I began to wonder what had happened to all the other people who had been whistling. Then it dawned on me that I was the only offender who had reported. As I reached for the door, John Mark, the Senior Prefect opened it and said, "Ah, were you whistling?"

"Yes."

"Right. Come in."

As I entered the bathroom I saw that all the school prefects were there – six House Captains plus the two or three who had not yet attained that rank: at least nine possibly ten. I do not remember the count. Evidently Mark had immediately decided to make this a major disciplinary issue, expecting many offenders to report from every house. Certainly, to judge from the loudness of the whistling noise this expectation was justified. All but one had fled. I quickly looked round this concentration of power. Where were the canes? Only Mark was holding one. It was long, clearly the notorious 'four-foot' (actually fifty-two inches).

Mark said at once, "I'm going to beat you, because it was very rude."

Peter Stirzaker was the first to react. He was my House Captain, and known to be my friend. I expected him to behave as if he hardly knew me and he came up to his best form at once: -

"Oh! Senior boy! He should get six, not just four. If he can't set an example at least we can."

I began to infer that they must have had some sort of discussion, probably deciding that, with a large number of boys reporting, the simplest procedure would be four strokes each, the House Captains taking turns.

Then D.G. Taylor (One North) echoed the same thought.

"Yes—should be at least six."

After a slight pause Nichols (Two North) said quietly:

"We were going to give them four all round."

So they had something of an anti-climax to deal with, in that only one of the many whistlers had reported for punishment.

Mark seemed to be prepared, and stood against the East wall of the bathroom. I had been in the middle of the room, silent and becoming more frightened by the second. The prefects were all on my left. (They had all used the urinal there; I had emptied my bladder just before reporting.)

Mark waited for any further comments. Finally he said:

"Right, you'll get five: Shorts only. Bend down." So, I prepared myself and went towards the nearest bath and started to bend down. He said:

"No, not that one; go further away, I want plenty of room. Now, you'll need to prepare yourself," he said, "by bracing your knees against the end of the bath. Take hold of the sides of it, reach out further in front, and you will need to rest your elbows on the sides as well."

Then there seemed to be a long, long pause.

Now these wily people had arranged to have beatings in One North bathroom because the process could be heard in it's entirety by three whole houses of boys out of six in the school. That meant half the school (about one hundred and fifty boys or more altogether). The other thing that was done was to leave the house room doors open, instead of having them shut during prep, just to make sure that everybody could hear clearly. I was quite determined that whatever else they heard, they would not hear my voice. It was generally agreed that the only way to get through this thing was to make the firm decision to not flinch, because if you started to move, you could break, and sure enough, every now and then somebody would fail and start screaming in between the last few strokes. This was always unpleasant. Rarely, a boy would break down completely, scream the place down and have to be held while the beating was completed. But, this didn't happen very often. When it did, there was always trouble. The parents would come and complain that they were not going to have their boy treated like this and that we had infringed his dignity or the school had done him some permanent harm.

I was holding my breath and the first stroke made me gasp in

a little. Then I couldn't breathe till at four I started to stand up. Mark said:
"No! One more."

The last one came and then the horrible sensation of pain actually increasing. On standing up slowly, I was shaking. After adjusting my dress I walked towards Mark to shake hands. I remember Peter Stirzaker catching my left arm to hold me, saying:

"Steady!"

I still have a clear picture in mind of Mark's hand stretched out towards me as I tried to connect with it.

I went outside the bathroom and propped myself against the wall. The door closed behind me. The school prefects were about five minutes longer, talking. I was several feet away and had no interest in hearing what was said. Then they filed out in silence. Last was Peter Stirzaker, still bright red in the face, and understandably so, since he had done his best to get one of his friends an extra two strokes and half succeeded. He took me by the arm to pull me off the wall and said:

"You went as white as a sheet in there. Your knees were giving way weren't they?"

"Just about, and you're still beet red in the face. Did you know?"

He let that pass.

"Better go to your study straight away and start prep. Are you going to be alright on the stairs?"

"Oh yes. I should be."

"Well, I'm going to the houseroom first. So come with me. It'll help if you walk." Then, when we were moving, he said:

"I should tell you – well it's obvious really – we were all glad you came and that you didn't break. Mark was certainly doing his best – quite a good best actually. And as for all the others…"

"Why should I care about them?" I interrupted rudely.

"That's right. It's not your business."

Peter just smiled and began to brighten up.

"They'll all begin to realize what they've done; and they'll all be frightened, if only for a short while and then when they wise up the best will feel guilty, and the others – Well. So what? They just have to live with it, don't they? So in a way their punishment is worse than yours. We're just going to forget them and leave it there."

I looked hard at him, while various possible smart answers went through my mind. Fortunately I was hurting too much and too frightened to say anything. He realized I was at least a little puzzled, pre-occupied by coping with the pain, then said:

"No, really, you just wait. A whole lot of good things may come out of this. At best, there should be a complete end to all the dreadful disorder in the thirds and middles – and not just Mr. Wicks' classes, but with Miss Simpson's forth form biology as well. She's having a hard time you know, and if only she had perfect order they'd find out what a good teacher she is. Five B is quiet."

We had been in Five B together three years before.

For the time being I was even more confused, and was still shaking my head in some disbelief as I opened the East houseroom door for him. I was thinking in terms of us not as friends but, as he had made so clear just ten minutes before, as school prefect and boy-who-needed-beating. So my mind filled with thoughts of, "What's wrong with him?" and "Why has he gone soft suddenly?" Most improper! He should brace up and remember he has to be House Captain and act like it." But even as I was thinking – he came up to form, swept into the room ahead of me, and I quietly closed the door behind us both. Beaumont, the senior house Prefect, taking prep at the time, immediately rose in deference and waited for Stirzaker to speak.

"This is Lines." He said, as if Beaumont needed informing. "He's been in One North bathroom with us, and we've settled some issues quite firmly."

So, he was already following up the action by making it as public as possible. One hundred and fifty boys had heard it. Now another fifty were officially informed. I was hoping I did not betray anything, although it would have been an offence to look up and study my face. I just stood by, waiting for Stirzaker to finish his errand. "Anyone late for prep?" he inquired.

"Oh yes, two on the list tonight! Plenty of others in a hurry and only just made it." I asked them –

"Any excuse?" and they both said:

"No!", so I left it there.

"That's all right. No need to quiz them. But make it six each, not just four."

"Very well, six each," said Beaumont, and Stirzaker made for the other houseroom door. The nearest boy jumped up and opened it for him, so that he was able to walk out quickly without breaking his stride. I followed and we walked together up two flights to the branch corridor where our sixth form study was just beyond the second for the East House prefects.

He said:

"Guess why they were late. Pretty obvious! But we'll see how they get on."

Then he went on to say carefully:

"Now, this is over as far as you are concerned – I mean the punishment part."

I again felt like responding, as I already realized that the healing would not be over for some weeks. My pants were feeling wet and sticky and the pain was lasting longer than I had expected.

"But now we have to make sure the whole school wakes up and shakes itself, and we have to reassure the teachers concerned. I think it will go well. You've been a help so far. So just think it over…"

"I'm sure I will." I said. "Thanks!"

This set the stage for what was to follow. But at the time I thought Peter's expectations were running too high. On reaching the study I realized it was only seven forty-five – total elapsed time about half an hour from the offence to the completion of punishment – efficient!

I entered the study to find the other three occupants facing their books but in fact discussing what they supposed had happened. M.J. Cross was a St. Nicholas scholar and had, as usual been at head table, so naturally had taken no part in the whistling. Little Phelps A.C., a perpetual goody-goody destined for high office in the church felt somewhat ashamed for the conduct of the whole school. The one other member, Gibson, from One North whose Housemaster Collinson regarded as a buffoon had whistled but not attended One North bathroom. So of the four, one was simply amused, one was vicariously ashamed, one ridden with guilt, and only I was feeling free, although still in the most horrible pain. I felt sorry for Gibson, although I was able to reassure him that there was no plan to root out any of the other offenders, as authority seemed satisfied that justice had been exhibited and the details would immediately be widely known. Also there was the certainty that those unpunished would bear the burden of their guilt. I could not help expressing how glad I was that I was fully cleared. Peter's words were unforgettable, and I began to realize that the prefects in general were now counting on me as their ally.

Thus, the beating was in no way a "Put down." It had rather sufficed to acknowledge the fact that a senior boy had unwittingly a silent following. It was hoped and expected that those younger boys who had seen me fall into disobedience would now be able to see me climb out as I had started to do. The whole process of accepting this system, harsh as it was, together with a punishment that was later proved to have been more severe than any of us had at first realized redounded more to my credit as time passed.

In the study I had difficulty returning to maths problems. The pain was deep and insistent and I remember that I was shivering with cold and I felt myself filled with a sense of fright which I could not understand as there was no guilt remaining. Later I understood that all this was caused by shock. In parallel with this was the happy understanding that I had some new friends at the apex of the hierarchy itself.

Soon, I began to feel sorry for John Mark as I felt sure that he had not intended to do me any permanent harm, although he would know that some scars would follow the use of that four foot cane. So I began to pray for him, especially that he should feel no guilt, having simply done his duty. Why did I do this? It seemed to come naturally to me, but must have been a prevenient grace, for I had thought that I was agnostic.

East House dormitory was in the old building, from the 1850's with access at the centre and one end; easily long enough to accommodate thirty beds and thirty small wardrobes each side and wide enough to allow about ten feet of clear walking space between the ends of the beds. The ceiling was high, framed in heavy timber and the windows, all at high level, were painted over jet black as part of the wartime blackout regulations. They could not be opened after dark until all lights were out. The floor was soft wood planking, planed and polished but not stained. In the centre was a bare wooden table.

So, by three minutes after nine p.m., every boy was seated on his bed facing the centre table for prayers, led by the house prefect for the week. Sometimes the Housemaster was there. There was a scripture reading, usually short, and then some evening prayers out of the Common Prayer book. One night Lieutenant C. Blackshaw turned up unexpectedly. Sutton was seen to be smiling to himself as he quickly changed his mind about the reading. He read Daniel III verses one to thirty, the tale of Nebuchadnezzar's image and the three children, rapidly without slip or hesitation. We had to congratulate him afterwards.

After prayers, the house prefect would order:

"Get undressed," and we did so quickly in silence. Then, "Speak." Was given, and we were free to talk, go to wash and jump into bed, by nine-thirty. The house prefect on duty would, at the nine-thirty bell, observe and loudly name anyone late or only halfway into bed. He would the pick up the clipboard, and read out for example:

"Janes Secundus four, hicks R.P. six." Adding any that he had had to name, then:

"Out of bed."

Every boy under this order would then jump out, bend over the end of his own bed and await the appointed number of strokes – delivered with a leather slipper. There were a few variations, such as having to bend over the centre table, or to describe the offence oneself, and sometimes a particularly boisterous boy might find himself on the list twice. It was never meant to be serious – although the prefect was required to do his best - really no more than a "brace-up" call. Most often there was no-one on the list at all. Finally, all these duties completed, the prefect would order: "Tuck under, lights out, open windows." Complete silence followed.

On this night, as soon as "speak" was given, the expected noisy banter started. Everyone had found out two facts-firstly, that I had been the only person beaten; secondly, that I had had five strokes. I was in too much of a hurry to get into the shower and cleaned up to pay much attention at the time, and just listened to things like:

"Hope it hurt, Lines."

"Was it that four footer? - I hope so"

"Yes it must have been – One North said it was about the loudest they'd ever heard."

"But it's the only time it's been used this term."

"Why did they stop at five? Couldn't they have dug up a few reasons for doing it properly?"

"Bet you stick to your pants for a few weeks, Lines."

"The four footer always scars you know."

"Yes! You're changed for life now. You'll never be the same again Lines."

"Serves you right! You could have just walked away like everyone else."

But, while showering off I couldn't hide it. Then the tone changed a little, and I began to hear:

"Bloody Hell! – Mark must be taking this seriously – did he take a run every time or what?"

I could answer that one. I had seen him start the first one from twenty feet away, and heard a few quick steps just as each whistle started.

"Just a few paces." I said

"Are they going after the others?"

"You're going to be buried with that Lines – for sure." Many a true word spoken in jest. And,

"Your friend Stirzaker must have really spoken up for you."

And a few just turned away, shaking their heads and saying:

"Bastards! Bloody Bastards."
And quite clearly:

"Well you know he and Stirzaker are pretty thick and they're all about the same age. So if that's what they do to their friends, what the....?"

This made me feel proud to know Peter Stirzaker, especially as the friendship was clearly firm as a rock. I was careful to avoid disclosing what part he had played in One North bathroom. They could imagine what they liked.

I was only just in time at the bell, and had put a folded towel in the bed, wearing no pants so that I would have dry underwear to wear in the morning. I had washed mine out in the shower and after wringing them hard, left them hanging to dry over night. Sleeping naked was common, as we were all growing fast, and clothes coupons could be used for garments more important than pajamas. I usually wore only underpants to bed.

So, at the nine-thirty bell, Beaumont picked up the clipboard, and announced the two names, and the offence.

"Late for prep, Six each, out of bed."

Beaumont was a large, likable person, with a talent for acting, and the ability to throw his booming stage voice easily throughout the large dormitory. He was about the same size as Mark, six feet two inches, and useful in the second row of the Rugger Fifteen. He was always on the lookout for a chance to play to the gallery, and as he approached the first bending subject, waving a slipper, he saw me rolling over carefully to watch and then smiling as I brought my hands out and rubbed them together. He stopped and looked at me and I saw his eyes twinkle; then, for all to hear:

"Lines! Are you really so cold that you have to rub your hands like that? I should have thought you were warm

-      Laughter all around –

"Silence!" from Beaumont. "I'm about to make all the noise we'll have here."

(A slipper makes a resounding clap, but does no harm whatever.)

He then went straight to the matter in hand, and as soon as he had completed it, called out loudly,

"Those by windows stand by! Tuck under! Lights out! Open windows!

Then when all was quiet: -loudly again:

"And sleep well you three!"

In fact I had little sleep that night. The towel kept the bed clean, but I had to peel it off in the morning. During the next few days I had comments from people I had hardly ever spoken to, especially in the houses that had heard the whole process so clearly.

"Congratulations Lines! You can whistle like three hundred people."

And,

"I'm sure I saw forty people in the corridor between One North houseroom and their bathroom. That was with about three minutes to go. I worked out we should hear at least a hundred strokes, and quite a lot of squealing. Then it all went quiet – just five but really loud."

"So you got all five did you? Not a sound – from you I mean."

"Thanks very much Lines! That was my beating you got there. Hope it hurt you enough – so that they can forget about me. I wouldn't really want it you know – I mean not enough to go and ask for it like you did."

And better still:

"Well Done Lines! Didn't know you had it in you."

All this was good natured and showed a great sense of solidarity in the school. There was indeed a realization that discipline had been breaking down and that respect for at least some of the teachers had needed firm restoration. There was also a sense of relief that in some way a need for just retribution had been met, and that the teachers in difficulty could be assured that disrespect had in fact been treated by exemplary punishment, which should be enough to frighten their troublemakers into better manners.

Mark followed up his actions on the Monday evening by visiting the Masters' Common Room the following day to convey the request that any boy behaving badly should be sent to him with a chit stating simply: "Disrespect." And signed by the teacher. The effect upon the classes was instant improvement, and no one misbehaved.

So, after having been somewhat subdued, I began to walk tall, if still carefully.

But Stirzaker was not letting it drop. On the Thursday, he and I happened to be walking in opposite directions in the crowded main corridor, when he hailed me loudly from several paces distant:

"Oh Lines – how's your bottom?"

I waited until we were closer, and said quietly,

"Bloody horrible! What's it meant to be like?"

But he intended to be heard.

"Just like that. So you mean it still hurts a good deal?"

"Yes!" I said, slowly, politely, but with some emphasis.

"Good! It was meant to. I thought it was a good beating."

Then, as he walked away he turned, saying loudly:

"So you won't forget it, will you?"
    "NO!" I said, just as loudly. He seemed determined to rub it in, in public. And the exchange had the desired effect-leaving me surrounded by people saying things like:

    "Jesus!"

And
"So he's your friend, is he? Still is?"

I found myself defending him vigorously;

"Yes, of course he's still my friend, and a good one, quite a fine character, in fact. You don't know him, do you?"

I was still determined to conceal what he had actually said.

Then, a boy from another house said:

"Lines, why must you be so bloody fair-minded all the time? Doesn't it strike you as unfair that you've just been sticked quite thoroughly and so many other people got away with nothing at all?"

I was riled by this.

"Haven't you got a few things wrong? One, I haven't just been sticked. It was... Oh! When was it? I forget."

Interruption – "Liar! You don't forget at all. It was three days ago exactly, and your own description is – I quote 'Bloody horrible',"

"OK. Three days ago. But, it wasn't all that thorough – only five remember, and it was not unfair."

"Why not? Of course it was, still is."

"Isn't it obvious?" I said; "Clear breach of discipline, disrespect for authority, shown by a senior boy in a public setting. Therefore it was followed by – what do you expect? Immediate severe punishment, of course, and it was meant to be exemplary. Now, what could be unfair about that? Don't you think everyone has behaved precisely as he should have done? And I mean – don't you think that includes me? Come on – Answer!"

"Well yes, and I'm glad you're so satisfied."

Quiet comment heard:

"Smug you mean."

"No, not quite 'satisfied'." I said, "Personally I've no reason to complain. But you're not using the right word. It's not 'satisfied', it's 'justified'. That does apply to me, completely, but not to anyone else. Now if that's what bothers you, perhaps there's something on your conscience. Why don't you unburden yourself.... to Mark for instance? You'll find him delighted to help. I mean he doesn't really need the exercise. He's in excellent condition. But I don't think that four footer has been used this term, until last Monday. Do give him the chance to practice a little. Perhaps that would make it more fair in your mind?"

Other remarks:

"This boy makes sense – just sometimes."

And,

"Hey Lines! Whose side are you on?"

One of them stretched out a hand:

"Damn you Lines! You're right, right for every bloody inch of that four foot. So thanks anyway, but I'm still lying low."

We shook hands warmly and I admitted to him:

"That was a bit harsh, I know, and I know I'm smug too. But it helps sometimes."

3 LITTLE A.J. AND PETER

That weekend one of the senior boys from West House, in fact J.A. Tait, younger brother to my friend and contemporary I.G. Tait, mentioned that one of the new boys in West was having nightmares, and I might be able to help him. I couldn't think how, and said so. He said:

"Well, about that thing on Monday night – do you remember anything about that?"

"Could I forget? I'll remember every damn detail for years, I'm sure."

"You're all right though, aren't you? It seems to have rolled clean off you."

"Well I wish it had. But no, it has not rolled off at all. The pain keeps coming back for no reason I know, and of course I'm having nightmares. Yes, maybe I roll over on it or something. But I wake up terrified and shaking just as I reach the door of One North bathroom- in the dream that is. Then the pain's there again. But it is such a relief to wake up. Funny! I wasn't shaking at all at the time, just frightened. Of course, if I'd had any idea what the pain was really going to be like I would have been totally terrified. But anyway, do you mean Little A.J.?"

"That's right. A.J. Lyne. And he talks of you as Big A.J."
"Yes, I know. That's how we greet each other sometimes. Nice kid, soprano. But he's so tiny! And he's still only twelve isn't he?"

"Only just twelve in fact. So could you talk to him?"

We arranged a meeting that afternoon on the North field and Little A.J. certainly looked unwell. He had been worried about having not turned up at One North bathroom on the previous Monday, and was frightened that he might be caught, and questioned about it.

"I'd have to own up because I was whistling and then I'd get caned, or punished for not being there, or both ... and I couldn't stand it..."

Poor little kid! He had it all wrong. We spent a long time while I was going over all the explanations that I had been giving to others, and he seemed to be a bit better. Then he mentioned Ellis. That was the clue.

Ellis, a cockney with an obvious accent, had been a new boy with A.J. at the beginning of that term. A.J. had naturally befriended him, an older boy, nearly fourteen, and in the same class – middle C, I think it was. Then Ellis committed some relatively minor misdemeanor that evidently merited the stick. This was not a long cane, but the little corporal's cane; about twenty-six inches, with a steel tip at each end. Ellis broke down completely and screamed and struggled long before it was finished. The attempt was finally abandoned. But the damage was done and, clearly he couldn't stay at school. Of course there was no sympathy from anyone, and he had boys saying things like:

"Glad you're leaving Ellis. We'll get some more peace during prep now."

And,

"Diddums hurtums itty bitty bottom then. Go home. Mommy kiss it better."

"Bye-bye Ellis – Good riddance…" and worse.

So I said:

"You had bad luck even knowing Ellis. You must realize he shouldn't have been here in the first place."

"Do you mean he wasn't tough enough? Well, neither am I."

He was on the verge of tears.

"Well, something like that but all sorts of other things as well. So, let's think about him for a bit. First, what does his father do?"
"He runs some kind of business. Ellis said it was a sales organization, and he said his Dad was always proud of being a 'self made man", as he put it."

"Nothing wrong with that really – and did you know that Flynn's Dad runs a dying and dry cleaning business – in Shoreham – owns it in fact – and I think Flynn plans to go into business as well – has to do accounting first. But - back to Ellis – he does talk cockney doesn't he? And Flynn doesn't. Have you heard any accents in the school at all?"

"No, but what harm does an accent do?"

"None at all, by itself, but it might be a hint of character. My Mother is a Cockney, yes really! You only have to be born within sound of Bow Bells. All her childhood she lived there. But she and her Mother never picked up a trace of accent. Both my Grandmothers came from Kent, sisters actually."

Little A.J. said: "How? I didn't think that was allowed."

"Oh, I don't know, perhaps it isn't, but they were. Funny! My Mother is quite a snob and whenever I asked what her

Grandfather did, she used to say: "Oh, we never tell anyone what he was." So for years I used to think, Pirate, Smuggler, Rumrunner, Slaver… and so on. Now she has told me he was a family butcher. What a lot of nonsense! Anyway my Grandmother speaks beautifully. So does Mother – But then she was trained – at the Royal Academy – for a mezzo soprano career. Enormous voice. In her early childhood she had been entertaining in the slums of SoHo and Lambeth, singing and dancing barefoot to a barrel-organ. So much for being upper class!

And another thing, Cockneys have wonderful loyalty to each other. They are known now as about the finest infantry in Europe, especially when they're properly led. We'll get to that."

Before he could question me I started off on another tack,

"What about your Dad – What does he do?"

"He's a Borough Surveyor. Says it's not very well paid. But it is a Government job."

"Do you know where he went to school?"

"Oh yes. He often talks about it – Sedberg. Says it was really primitive and much too tough. That's why he didn't want me to go there. Said Cranleigh would be a more gentle place. But it doesn't look that way to me now – not for you anyway."

"Oh, don't start that again – after all, I'm seventeen now, and you're only just twelve. I couldn't possibly have stood up to it at your age. You must know most new boys are thirteen…But then Sutton was twelve."

"Anyway, as for Sedberg – It's tough because of where it is. It's in the middle of Yorkshire, miles from anywhere.

Windswept, cold – It's like Wuthering Heights country. Have you read that yet?"

"No, what's it about?"

"Oh, it just about makes you freeze to read the book. I think you'll find it's required reading in the Middles." I tried to get back to the idea of leadership.

"So, look. There are five years of growing between you and me. And you are starting out tougher than I was at your age. Do you realize? I was even a bit older than you are now when the war started. I remember that so clearly. It was a fine Sunday morning; I was out on the Downs with our little dog. He was trying to catch rabbits, but was never fast enough. It was blackberry time. Then the air-raid sirens began. I thought: 'Clever Germans! They must have been just longing for this.' So I was listening for bomb sounds. Nothing happened. It had been some Observer Corps trainee who couldn't identify an Anson. Imagine! Thought it was a Heinkel. They are nowhere near alike. Then the 'All-clear' sounded as I reached home. I found all the family gathered round the wireless with long faces, talking about Neville Chamberlain's speech. These are marvelous days to live in you know. May not be another war for twenty years or more."

A.J. told me what he could remember, and how his Dad was so sad that he was in a reserved occupation, or too old or both so wouldn't be able to join up and how his Mother had seemed so upset that he was thinking like that.

I said: "But that's the way men do think, isn't it? At least public school men do. Not like the working classes. Do you know what happens in war? It is always the same. You never see a public school man getting called up – because they all volunteer. And what do you see, or hear about the Old

Cranleighans? – Well not much 'til you hear another one's been killed, or missing or something. And they're not killed doing clerical work, or as aircraft fitters. No, those are not the glory things. But you won't hear anyone talk about glory either. They just seem to follow their instincts and go for the action – fighter pilot, bomber command, submarines, tank corps, commandos, and so on. Actually I'm applying for Fleet Air Arm – you know, String Bags and all that – and Sunderlands now. Beautiful aircraft! They're based on the old C class of Empire Flying Boats – Bristol Pegasus engines.

Now, instinct – what is it that makes you or me, (like your Dad) – want to go straight for the services in emergencies? I mean the really active services – while all the working class young men, or it seems, most of them, wait 'til they're called up and even then try to do the easy things? Can you see why it happens?"
"No! Not really. But you're making it sound disgraceful to be called up. Perhaps it is. I know I'd rather volunteer."

"So, there you are!" I said, "You are thinking like a normal public school boy – or man, or whatever we are, already. So this is what I meant by saying, 'when they're properly led' – I didn't let you in to the discussion just then. You're ever so polite, you know, "I started laughing.

"But yes." Now I could open up about the leadership thing and he would find himself assenting – really by nature. "Do you realize that you – you will be one of the leaders?"

"In a way I'd like it, but that's way, way ahead surely!"

"Yes, it is years away. But just look what happens to people at public school. You can't help but become wonderfully fit, almost without trying – I mean compared to a working class boy at the same age. By the time you're half-finished here you'll be slick at all the drill and weapons training. The discipline won't bother you a bit. This is worse than the army – did you realize?

Now, there's no privilege about joining from a public school. You are going to be on level ground with a huge majority of working class conscripts. And just because of the way you speak they are bound to try to put you down. But that doesn't last long, because it's competition all the way and they don't even realize that. So while they're griping, cursing the army or whatever service it is, you will be happily polished up, neat, cheerful, all your drill moves perfect. You'll do exactly as you're told; never crack your expression – just like you've learned here. You'll cope with obstacle courses and U.A.C. easily ahead of your squad. You might find you can beat your P.T. instructor home on a run. All sorts of things like that. After a march with a twenty pound pack, they'll probably come home exhausted and cursing. You'll be laughing, saying, 'Oh yes! Five miles today with twenty pounds so by good army logic it should be ten miles tomorrow with forty pounds.' Then you jolly the stragglers along, and if a man twists his ankle you might help him home. So you drop him at the Platoon Commander's feet and salute smartly."

"Casualty Sir. Ankle I believe."

"Thank you Private Lyne. Assist him to sick bay."

"Yes Sir. Sick bay." And salute again.

"You do exactly as you are bid. You get noticed. You get followed by others because you can't help doing things better and quicker than they do. Then promotion starts, by merit entirely. It always works. They will know you deserve it. It just follows. See?"

"Yes." he said, "I don't feel like much of a leader now though."

"Never mind – just wait and carry on, and grow of course." We both laughed at this; "You're just bound to do the right thing, almost by instinct, in an emergency. Somehow it's in the blood. It is amazing what people rise to – I mean anyone. Do you know about the man in Q-Turret on Beatty's flagship – Lion at Jutland?" He shook his head.

"Well Lion was thin-skinned on top like all the British battle cruisers. Suddenly there was a fire flashing right into the ammunition lift. This man saw the danger, and despite his own mortal wounds, reached the voice pipe and ordered: "Close watertight doors. Flood the magazine." All the magazine crew under Q-Turret (that was two thirteen-point-five), drowned in seconds. But he had saved the ship. Three other battle cruisers, including Queen Mary, sister ship to Lion, had blown up that way, that day. Amazing! How do people come up with the right action, suddenly, like that? But I suppose it can happen to anyone – You, for instance."

"Well isn't that what happened to you on Monday? No one else did it."

"It wasn't difficult you know. People exaggerate."

"So, why did you faint?"

"Who told you that? Anyway I didn't, I just nearly did."

"Well I heard Tait J.A., and the West House prefects talking about it."

I didn't know how to laugh that one off. But he was much more cheerful. So I just had to say,

"Well if you had been there you wouldn't have had anything like that. They would have scaled everything down for your age and your size. They're quite reasonable people, really. And growing up is a slow process. So does that help at all?"

It seemed to.

"And as for Ellis – He didn't have the stuff in him. This is really why the working classes will never take over public schools, and why they hardly ever even try to get scholarships into them. They can't stand the discipline. They preach at each other constantly about everybody having his own personal dignity, about being just as good as the next man. But really dignity is earned, like the man in Q-turret – he got a posthumous V.C. – and as for being as good as the next man – O.K., perhaps it holds up 'til the next man just seems to be better than them at most things. Then they discover he's out of some public school – not always of course. So, when Ellis broke down he had his parents to blame and all their friends in that class for the way he'd been brought up – brainwashed – for years."

We said nothing for a while. Then I thought it time to soften up.

"So, you've known all along that I'm not tough at all inside. And yes, I did just about faint. And yes, it was horrible. I'm glad I had no idea beforehand what it was going to be like. And, do you know? I'm getting nightmares too. I wake up just as I'm getting to One North bathroom. I'm shaking and sweating; I was telling Tait J.A. about that. It's such a relief to wake up. But it's a physical thing. I'm sure it'll all go away when it's healed over."

Again, he was starting to look as if he was sorry for me.

"So, first of all, do you realize you have nothing whatever to worry about? It really is over, for all time. They are not even thinking of punishing anyone else." But he hadn't tumbled to it.

"Why not? Everybody else still feels guilty. They say they don't and some of them even resent the fact that you got all the punishment they gave out."

"Well, they shouldn't. It's not as if I was punished for anyone else. Look at it from the outside. It's an example thing. I'm seventeen, should be setting a good example - didn't. You can compare it to executing the leader of a gang. The others vanish. In this case, if by beating one you can terrify three hundred – don't you think that's efficient? The whole school needed a wake-up and got it. Poor Mr. Wicks! I hear he's a good teacher. Isn't he?"

"Well his classes are so quiet now, and he is quite interesting."

"So that's just what was wanted – it worked."

"But I still feel guilty."

"Forget it! And if it was ninety percent to do with example, you're not concerned at all. You don't have to set any kind of example. Just find a few good ones and follow them. Your turn will come. Only don't do what I did." But I had to stop that line of thought.

"So, no need for any nightmares. Nothing bad is going to happen. It's all happened and over. By the way, do you know I worked out timing? – From the offence till the end of the beating must have been about twenty minutes. Ten minutes later I was at work on maths again - at least, trying. How's that for efficiency?"

I had to thank him for letting me get all this off my chest. It had been a help to be able to talk and clear my own mind about it. So, at seventeen and just over twelve, we had been able to help each other. As we separated he looked much happier and I certainly was. But it was too far-fetched to compare my action with that of the illustrious Major Harvey, V.C., of Lion, 1916.

That was the Saturday. Next day, Matins and Evensong as usual; all were in their places, functioning as expected. Little A.J. was in the front row, soprano stalls, South side facing North. Sutton was in a tenor spot, back row South side facing North. I was singing bass parts, back row North side facing them both and having to share music with Nichols, tenor, the Two North House Captain, who had been the sole voter for four strokes six days before. The four-part male choir of about thirty was a beautiful sound. Little A.J. clearly enjoyed it. We smiled briefly at each other once or twice. I felt privileged.

I had not clearly observed the older man in the visitors' pews. There were often old O.C.'s whom we could not identify, visiting out of pure nostalgia. It was, I learned later, Little A.J.'s father.

During the week following at last my friend Peter Stirzaker began to look better. Something had been bothering him and I told him he had looked bad.

"Just a flu." He said.

"Well, I felt rotten too and reported sick. So she took my temperature and looked at my records. Then put me off sports for this week. I have to see her tomorrow. Actually I need the time to study."

"Your ass is still wide open. Isn't it? You didn't show her that?"

"No, you bet I didn't!"

Peter understood what was happening. I had been sleeping badly and for several days had no sense of hunger but some nausea at meal times. He had seen that I was unwell and at English and Divinity periods, when we usually sat side by side, he was quietly solicitous, often saying "Careful" as I sat down slowly.

On looking back to the period, it should be born in mind that I must have been under some physical stress. I had only recently started to ignore all previous medical advice which had been to avoid over-exertion since a period of ill-health from age 7 to 10 ½. Then there was the wartime malnourishment, coming at the time of a normal growth spurt, so that recovery from the trauma of punishment was not as rapid as it should have been. However, this understanding does not detract from my respect for Mark's expertise with the stick.

"When is your qualifying exam?" He asked.

"Just after Easter, I have to take it in Cambridge. I didn't realize that Engineering was all maths and that's all this is. One paper is pure and the other is applied. It is usually taken in second year. So it'll be difficult."

"Do you think you have a chance?"

"Oh yes, I expect I'll pass it. I've never failed an exam yet."

He stood back and grinned:

"You haven't changed much have you? Conceited as ever."

"Oh I have, I have. You're never the same again, remember?"

I was of course alluding to the scars, and although we both laughed a little, Peter slowly nodded in understanding.

"When is your Inter B.Sc.?" I said.

"Not 'til September."

"Well you should be O.K. It's pretty well the same as Higher Certificate."

"Are you doing Higher again this year?"

"Yes, I'll be the youngest Higher in Science from this school for the second year running. But I don't really need it now. So I can concentrate on pure and applied maths."

"Well, I'll be doing Engineering Drawing and a whole lot of other things – like reading Kipling: You know the Ballad of East and West?"

I said,"Oh East is East and West is West and never the twain shall meet
'Til earth and heaven stand presently at God's great judgment seat."

We said the refrain together.

"For there is neither East nor West, border nor breed nor birth
When two strong men stand face to face though they come from the ends of the earth"

"Yeah," I said. "And in the same ballad":
"You could hear a breech bolt snick where never a man was seen."

"My Father knows all about that. He was a junior engineer up there on the N.W. Frontier during the Khyber Pass railway construction, about '99. There was a disturbance, and several of Her Majesty's servants were shot at – the "at" is the important word, you understand. They were not really trying to kill people. But one of Father's Hindu staff came to him…

"Lines, Sahib, my wife and all my children need me now. This place very dangerous. I must have leave of absence at once." Etc…

The tribesmen making the trouble were Pathans – fine big men, fair or red hair – descendants of Alexander's Greeks and Macedonians; and all Muslim. So the Hindus had cause for alarm. But Lines Sahib opened his desk drawer to show his revolver.

"I am a servant of Her Majesty. This gun is loaded." (So it was, at all times). "You will stay at your post, and any man who does not will come under the orders of military law."

Of course he had no authority to say this.

That night he heard the unmistakable "snick" of a breech bolt, looked out from his bungalow and at first saw nothing. As his eyes became accustomed to the night he made out a guard of Pathans, facing away from his house. They were guarding him. They had no time for Hindus. But Lines Sahib was behaving as a good servant of Her Majesty and needed protecting. In the morning they declared themselves to him openly, smiling broadly, and took their leave. That disturbance settled quickly when the tribesmen called it off and melted away into their rocky fastnesses. Nothing material achieved. But they had terrified some Hindus and again earned the respect of the British.

And have you read the one about the old Scottish sea engineer? He's a Calvinist and it shows him so clearly, half asleep on watch as he gazes at his crossheads, predestined to move up and down in their guides for ever. I wish I could remember it."

He hadn't found this one yet. After thinking for a while he said, "When was the Afghan War then? Kipling wouldn't remember that would he?"

"I don't know the dates of it. But he's not long dead; died in '36."

"When you're wounded and left on Afghanistan's plains"

Then he joined in:
"And the women come out to cut up what remains
Just roll to your rifle and blow out your brains.
And go to your Gawd like a soldier."

I said:

"My friend Merrick Johnson, born in Poonah, said his Father was in it as a Subaltern, in the Pioneers, a regiment raised to man one or more of the Khyber Pass forts. His Major forbade him to ride his usual conspicuous white horse. So Johnson painted it with potassium permanganate solution, expecting it to go brown (manganese dioxide). But it did not – it just remained a brilliant pink, much to the amusement of the officers' mess. Johnson was due to retire on first September 1939. When the war was declared on the third, he volunteered. The reconstituted pioneers were cooks and quartermasters. Johnson was captured at St. Valerie."

Peter was staring at me and starting to laugh.

"What's up?" I said.

"John Mark, Nichols, Tait I.G. and I were just talking the

other day and we agreed all this couldn't have happened to a better person. I had to tell you that."

"All this – all what? Well I know what. But am I meant to feel honoured, or...? And don't worry. There are just not going to be any repeats you know."

"I mean the way you are taking it. And your sense of humour has helped the whole school, even including the Masters' Common Room. The explanations you've given out – They're just bang on – honestly!"

"Really! I haven't found it funny. But I'm happy to have been so useful." (Sarcastically) "After all, if I hadn't had a sense of humour to put things back in proportion, life could have been dreadful. I'll never forget some of the things you said, - especially that time on Thursday..."

He was laughing.

"That's good" He said again. "You won't forget it, will you...?"

Just the same tone and intonation as before, and just as loudly, "...ever?" But we were both laughing this time. "Impossible!" I said, and then the thought struck me suddenly:

"How did you manage to get all the way through school and you never had it? You old rogue! No scars on your ass-piece and you must have deserved it at some time. Perhaps it's just as well you never knew what it was like. Might have made you too soft – and you wouldn't have behaved with such splendid impartiality in One North bathroom. No! On second thoughts I don't think it would have made the slightest difference."

"Exactly!" He said. "You have a thing to do, and you do it. You showed us that alright. You should have heard some of the things said in that bathroom after you had left."

"Amazing! And I was trying to stand up outside. Feeling – well apart from the pain – just a flood of admiration for the way you had spoken up immediately. Not a hint of hesitation or favouritism or anything. Do you realize that's the best thing you could have done for me – just your plain duty."

"That's what I was going to get to about the Ballad of East and West. Don't you think it reflects us a little?"

"Well, we're not exactly 'strong men' – not yet, or not me. I was just explaining all that to Little A.J. on Saturday. Did you know I'm getting nightmares?"

"Oh yes, The other night you suddenly said: 'Yes' –then sat up in bed, looked round and said 'Bloody Hell' – 'Oh Thank God' and went to sleep again straight away - I doubt if you'd fully woken up. Ian Tait and I had both been woken up by it. We laughed as you lay down again, - it seemed totally at peace. Ian said; 'I bet I know where he was in that dream.' He'd seen you do it before, sometimes a few times in one night."

"Ah! So that's what made him say: 'Did you sleep alright Alfred? You were restless'."

"I knew I had been awake at times. Ian told me I looked as if I'd been up all night. In fact I've had pretty poor nights. And last Monday – well I'm sure I was awake at every hour – just had cat naps. That's why I didn't think I'd be able to help Little A.J. much, because he so needed a big strong elder brother. That Ellis creature had been quite wrong for him. You know I'm glad he didn't turn up on Monday. It would have been awful. He's so small. Anyway I'm sure we helped each other. I don't mind a bit if he knows I'm a weakling inside. So, there you are – I'm not a strong man really – not yet anyway."

He said:

"Well! Don't worry about it. You damned well perform like one. As for the 'ends of the earth' part – we've both got our feet planted firmly on English sod. But we have come from opposite ends of a long cane." Again, we were able to laugh easily at this and as we did so we realized that my tenor friend, Nichols (of Two North) was joining in and had heard most of what we had been saying. He said:

"So now I know what keeps you two engineers together. It's quoting poetry to each other."

But I was getting serious. I explained carefully: -

"Do you know what I think it is? We've each behaved bang up to the other's expectations or better. It's been difficult but in some way automatic and it gives you such confidence to know you can trust someone. Funny! But there it is."

"Yeah," Peter said: "I believe he's got it right." We walked into hall together.

BLACKSHAW

On Friday of that week, when I was just recovering, beginning to heal and to sleep better, the Housemaster called me into his study after lunch. He seemed quite cheerful and welcomed me into a chair opposite him, so that we sat facing each other across his desk. He made small talk for a few minutes, asking about my intended career in the Royal Corps of Naval Constructors with its two possible routes of entry.

During the previous year, I had competed at Fareham for entry to a Dockyard School and found that fifty-four out of over a thousand had been accepted, of whom I was number forty-six. But there were three other dockyards, and by serial eliminating competition there would remain only two from all four dockyards at final entry to Royal Naval College, Greenwich. I found the odds too fierce so I opted for the other avenue, starting with a Mechanical Sciences Tripos at first or second class honours level. Meanwhile I had sent in papers to volunteer for Fleet Air Arm Training. Blackshaw was meant to be Careers Advisor for all of us: but in fact knew very little about industry. He had been no great help to Peter Stirzaker. I had been advised by my Father and by Rev. D.G. Loveday, our Headmaster, though I had always imagined that he would have preferred to see Cranleigh Scholars as Dons, teaching Latin, Greek, Hebrew and Divinity in Oxford and Cambridge Colleges.

But Charles came to the point:

"Lines, it's very clear that you have qualities that we need to recognize and if I may say, reward. You are really overdue for some serious responsibility, you know. How do you feel about that?"

"I'm sure I could deal with it adequately, Sir. It does seem that often enough when I start to talk people tend to shut up and listen."

"We need you on side, Lines! You know people follow character. Just now England needs men, not afraid of instant decision, able to lead against odds. I'll say no more. But I hear you're thinking of volunteering. I thought you were going to Cambridge for engineering. You could get deferment with a brain like yours, like a shot. – And with your medical record you probably won't be accepted anyway for active service."

"Yes, I know Sir. But I'm hoping for Fleet Air Arm, if the war lasts long enough. I've sent in the papers. The medical and the interview come up in the summer."

"Splendid! Well, you'll be hearing more, and quite soon I believe. So, do your best! – That's all for now."

Evidently either Stirzaker or Mark had been talking to him, or maybe some of the other teachers. This meant house prefect status. "About time!" I thought.

4 MISTAKE

Just two days later, on the Sunday afternoon, I happened to be walking towards the Bell site at the junction with the main staircase when a boy of about sixteen, I think from One and Four South, approached from the other direction. He had been amongst those who, ten days before had heard and seen the whole of that now famous challenge by Peter Stirzaker. As he started to climb up the stairs towards his own houseroom, he turned back towards me and said, in a remarkably good imitation of Peter,

"Oh Lines, how's your bottom?"

I laughed and said:

"Doing well. At least it's dry now, some of the time."

But he started talking about how I had been used so unfairly as an object lesson and should resent it. Obviously he had missed the point. I didn't feel like going into it all again and said:

"Well just suppose no one had turned up at all! Personally, I'm glad that they found one person they could jump on." (I had often wondered what Mark would have done if no-one had answered his summons to One North Bathroom.) "It seems to have done what was needed. Just look at Miss Simpson's biology, or talk to any of the Middles and think about Mr. Wicks. They like him now."

"You could have just turned round and walked away like we did instead of pushing through by yourself."

That was enough. I said:

"You won't even survive the war. You'll be shot, blindfold and alone."

Almost certainly he would not recognize the poetic allusion, "I could not look on Death, which being known men led me to him blindfold and alone" (R. Kipling). But his face changed to anger. He knew what was meant. I could not resist the temptation to drive that one home, and as he went upstairs, called after him: -

"Oh! Did that hurt? Good! It was meant to; and you won't forget it. Will you?"

It was a really good imitation of Peter. But it had been heard by others.

At the vestry, before Evensong, I was much too early. But following me closely was Nichols, Two North. As we reached the door he said:

"Lines, your voice is very clear and carries well. I heard it from the Quad – at least, just outside Hall. Now remind me, what were you caned for just thirteen days ago?" He was his school prefect self now, rather than my tenor friend.

"Disrespect for authority." I said.

"Just as well you got that right! I was beginning to wonder if you remembered. And wasn't it disrespect to your House Captain – to imitate him – mock him in fact, like that?"

"Yes."

"So – You've done exactly what you did before. Haven't

you? What do you think happens now?"

"That's not my business is it?"

"It's not for you to decide – but it certainly is your business. I mean… What do you think should happen to you?"

I was frightened already and the pain was with me again.

"It depends whether you laugh and just forget it – in which case nothing. Or take it seriously. In that case – well – you tell me."

"I haven't told anyone else 'til now. But someone else has told Mark, and he is taking it seriously. Quite honestly, I'm not surprised. How can we just forget it and laugh? Now what do you think you can expect?"

"Looks bad when you put it together – so, more of the same I suppose."

"Well, Mark and a few others are thinking 'the same only more so.' We're called to a meeting on it after Evensong. So I would expect action tonight."

By this time the vestry was filling up with boys changing into standard black cassock, and white surplice. The choir director came in to say that we were going ahead with the Walmisley in D minor Magnificat and Nunc Dimittis, and that as usual there were only twenty copies for the choir of over thirty. We had rehearsed this well and loved it. It is one of the most popular settings in the Cathedrals and Schools - and not difficult. Everyone enjoyed it as much as ever. Nichols and I paired up well as tenor and bass out of the same copy. I'm sure no one had any idea what we had been talking about.

Afterwards, in the vestry: -

"How did it go Little A.J.? You enjoyed it. Didn't you?"

He was almost a caricature of a pink faced choir boy in his cassock and short surplice, and even more so on days when we did an introit, like "Lead Me Lord" – carrying his music well up so that he could sing out with his head erect while reading it. He said, "It is beautiful music. Isn't it?"

Evensong ended about six fifteen. Nichols hurried away to his meeting. Supper was at six forty-five, lasting until about seven fifteen. "Action" could come at seven thirty, or soon after.

Sundays were different in many ways. At seven thirty there was a bell, not for prep, but for "Lock ups." Boys had to be in houserooms or studies by that time and again there was a nine o'clock bell to signal the move to the dormitory.

Details of that School Prefects meeting I gleaned later that term from Nichols and Mark mainly. First Mark read out his catalogue of offences. –

"Shouting in the main corridor,
Up the main staircase: -
Using words and tone of voice to mimic exactly
Or rather mock – a school prefect.
In fact, his House Captain.
All this by a senior boy
Already acknowledged as an exemplar to others
Compounded by the fact that it was a second offence
Identical to that for which he was punished thirteen days
ago."

Some of the school prefects could not help laughing

aloud at this elaborate analysis. Mark did not see the funny side, and gave his opinion immediately.

"All this means, firstly, that the first punishment was not adequate so that Stirzaker's suggestion of six strokes should have been followed: secondly, especially since the good achieved by the first beating might now be undone completely, in the school at large, I mean, - this time it must be more stern, probably eight: thirdly, Stirzaker should do it, with all the school prefects making it clear that this is the way we want it done."

At this, Stirzaker apparently baulked, saying:

"No! For one thing no one else can do it anything like as well as you can. You know that yourself. For another, I'm his friend, and I really would prefer not to – surely people would be able to find fault, one way or another. No! It ought to be a perfectly impersonal thing."

Nichols told me later that he had been firmly in agreement on both these points and so had some of the others.

Meanwhile the laughing minority held their ground, seeking reasons to reduce the penalty. All sorts of things were said:

"Doesn't he have a weak heart?"

"You won't finish it anyway, because he nearly fainted last time, so this time it's bound to hurt more because it's still clearly visible, - not even properly healed over yet, and he'll pass right out at three or four. Then what?"

"Then in the houserooms they'll hear it stop at three and say or think, 'This means Stirzaker's done some persuading this time. He's getting away with less'."

Nichols pointed out to them all that in fact I had not fainted, only nearly did, and that not until afterwards. So he brightly suggested that Mark could still get eight strokes in if he could just not take so long in between, and they should keep my head down, or pour cold water over my head to stop me from fainting anyway.

"If you faint just when the pain is at its worst, it loses its point, doesn't it?"

Mark was having his own doubts by now and asked: "Peter, what's it like now? Is it healed over?"

Peter thought hard but realized that he had to let the truth be known.

"No! It is not. Nowhere near. Just a lot of black scabs and crusts; and as soon as a stick hits it, it'll break open and you'll have blood all over the place. That's never happened before."

"Better drop the stick idea." Said Mark. Others agreed.

Of course the One North House Captain had to say:

"Oh yes! What a concept! Splatters of East House blood all over One North bathroom! How revolting! Can't have that!"

This brought laughter and the whole meeting brightened up still more when someone said quietly:

"Slipper!"

Nichols told me that even Stirzaker and he began to feel

relieved, and they all realized that they might be taking the whole thing, including them, too seriously.

Mark summed up: -

"So, one, no stick. He's had enough pain already and it would do only harm if we were seen to be callous or cruel or anything.

Two, he doesn't get away with it. So we'll go the publicity route this time. Half the school heard the first beating..."

"Very clearly, in fact, in all three houserooms" – interruption by two of the House Captains.

"And now we can have the whole of East House see the slippering.

"Three, we can put it on to East House prefects to demand respect for their House Captain by coming up with a written sentence for your list tonight, Peter. You or I can just countersign it. Can you get to that straight after Hall?"

Someone said: - "Bare bottom." (The Major managed the Ds in this way.)

Mark said firmly:

"No! O.K., supper time. I think that will finish it up."

Meanwhile, I had heard nothing official since the brief talk with Nichols before chapel. In the short time before supper I had been trying, without much success, to concentrate on maths problems. Sheer fright and that pain kept intruding.

At supper the word was passed that all the East House

prefects and Lines were to convene in the first study at seven fifteen. This small room was used by Stirzaker, Tait and Beaumont. Fitting in six people was a squash. Nobody sat.

Stirzaker opened it,

"Lines, you know what this is about. So does everyone else. I understand Nichols was talking to you. We've decided to go for publicity rather than pain this time for some good reasons. Lucky for you! This means you will have all the attention on tonight's list, and I'm now asking the house prefects to go into the second study and write out their recommendations. You stay here for now."

He handed Mark's list of the offences to Tait who, as house prefect for the week would chair the meeting next door. Ian turned to me saying:

"Lines for someone so intelligent, how can you spoil it by being such an idiot?"

When they had gone Stirzaker said:

"What you say to me in private and what you say in public have to be different. You should know that. I mean I don't care two hoots personally. But in public – Oh no! So of course you have to be punished. You were quoting Kipling. Why didn't you leave it there?"

"I know. I realize all that especially after what Nichols was saying before chapel. But I did it and it doesn't help anyone for me to say I'm sorry. One thing worries me. You're not letting yourself down, are you? I mean I was honestly expecting much worse after the way Nichols was talking."
He was silent. I said:

"So don't do anything you might reproach yourself for –

Why don't I just shut up? – I don't have to tell you that. You'll do what you like. – I'm sorry, I don't really mean that either."

I took a deep breath. "I'm trying to say that I trust you to say and do exactly what you see as your duty. No personal bias whatever. Boy! Have I got a big mouth?"

He was nodding quietly in the affirmative with a trace of a smile.

Tait came in with the recommendation. It was for six with a slipper at nine thirty that night, by Beaumont.

Stirzaker took it from Tait, changed the six to eight, signed it and passed it to me.

"You'll be reading this aloud tonight." He said. "Now sign it yourself."

I looked through it quickly, and saw that he had raised the stakes a little.

"So you've come up to scratch. I have to do the same." I said, and duly signed my name under his.

"You'd better." He said, smiling at me as I turned to leave. I heard him say:

"You will." As I shut the door.

These few words and the simple instant change of six to eight together with the flash of a friendly smile confirmed my confidence in him. I knew that I, in turn, would not let him down. I spent the evening trying again to take my mind off the inevitable by thinking hard about maths. I could not help but feel thankful that my nightmares were not going to be fulfilled. But I knew Beaumont would be in his element.

BEAUMONT

In the dormitory, Peter Stirzaker came through the West end door followed by all the house prefects, just before nine thirty. Beaumont waited for the bell, and then said, in his clear stage voice;

"Can everyone see and hear from that end?"

Calls of:
"Yes" From the East end. Then: -

"Lines! Your voice carries very well, as you no doubt realize. So now, use it.
Read this loudly, slowly and carefully. Everyone must hear it all."

He handed me Mark's catalogue of the offences, now finishing with:-

"Eight of the best with a slipper in East House dormitory after the nine thirty bell, laid on by Beaumont, Senior House Prefect."

I was careful to read it exactly as ordered, and thought the essential procedure would follow at once. But Beaumont savoured the suspense.

"Lines, are you quite confident that all these charges are true?"
"Yes!" – Loudly.

"And are you confident that the punishment is appropriate?"

"Yes."

"And adequate?"

This took me by surprise, and I was slow to respond.

"Yes."

"You seem hesitant. Whose signatures do you see at the bottom?"

"P.S. Stirzaker, A.J. Lines and J.N. Mark."

"And who is named to carry out this punishment?"

"Yourself, Beaumont, Senior House Prefect – I did read that already."

"Ah, yes. You did. And do you expect me to do my best?"

"It is clearly ordered that you shall. You have no option."
"Correct. Now bend down, and count out loud."

There followed the appointed number, and I was relieved to find how little pain there was. But I weakened on the count, and "seven" was quiet. By "eight" I had no breath left, and just as I was thinking...

"Not too bad! I can breathe again now." Suddenly – BANG! And a new, really sharp pain.

"Nine" I shouted, jumping up and turning to face Beaumont who had been on my left, (being right handed). At that instant I realized he had done it out of pure mischief, so I contrived a smile. My voice had certainly come back to full volume.

"Oh dear! I just didn't hear you say 'eight'." Said Beaumont.

"Quite right! I don't remember saying 'eight' myself."

"Ah! So we had a share, as it were, in the miscount."

"Oh no! My fault entirely, I'm sure. I should have been counting aloud and couldn't finish."

I was still smiling a little at his idea of harmless fun. We had both continued this exchange at stage voice production level. However, with the last crack, taken as I had just started to move, Beaumont had opened up something. (Fortunately, perhaps by his intention, all the previous eight had struck well above the painful area). I now felt a warm trickle down my right thigh, and then a few tiny splashes onto the back of the right heel.

Beaumont dropped the slipper onto the floor, and said as loudly as ever.

"So! Cast–iron backside, Lines!"

I changed my expression to stony hard, and said, slowly and as icily as I could:

"No. Cast-iron does not bleed."

"Oh! Is it bleeding?"

I said: "Yes, you could expect it to. Wasn't that the intention? I'm sure our House Captain would have been disappointed if you hadn't done your best."

I stepped back revealing a little puddle, and saying:

"Do be careful where you tread."

I turned my back to him. He did just as I was hoping, putting his hand to his head, and saying:

"Oh! My hat! You'd better get a towel and get cleaned up."

I had been waiting for this favorite expression of his, and said:

"Oh yes. Thanks! I will. But I think your hat was blown away on Ilkley Moor, wasn't it?" (Tha's goin to catch thy death o'cold... Then we shall 'ave to bury thee... on llkley Moor bhat 'at...on lkely Moore bhat 'at...)

Titters of laughter followed.

"Silence!" There was immediate attention. "Now does everybody understand what can happen when you show disrespect for authority?"

Chorus of –"Yes".

"So; you won't forget it, will you?"

I thought, "Poor Peter! He'll never live that down."

Once in the bathroom I heard Beaumont say:

"Tuck under, lights out, open windows."

The bleeding was only from where some scabs had cracked away, and soon stopped. I washed out my pants and left them hanging over a shower to dry overnight, then slung my towel over one shoulder and walked back, otherwise quite naked, through the darkened dormitory to my bed near the West end. The other house prefects and Peter had left. There was dead silence as I walked back through the dormitory, knowing that all eyes were trying to study my rear end. I sensed the respect for dignity that was truly earned.

Beaumont was still there. I smiled at him sincerely, as our eyes became accustomed to the dark, and placed the towel in the bed, folded with cleanest side to lie on. I really felt like congratulating him. Then he said, loudly again:

"Sick bay tomorrow Lines, eight fifteen."

I returned to stage form:

"Do I have to? It's going to heal anyway, and I really don't need Nurse Laurie to kiss it better. I mean – can't we keep the women out of this?"

"Dear Boy! She won't kiss it better. She'll put tincture of Iodine on it – liberally – probably rub it in – gentle creatures these nurses, aren't they! And of course it is a rule that every wound or scrape that bleeds has to be reported to sick bay. We don't want it getting infected now do we? Really Lines, you must understand that we all care about your bottom. I'm sure the whole school knows your House Captain inquires after its health from time to time."

That round a clear win to Beaumont.

Again, titters from all over the dormitory.

"Silence!" He roared again, obviously relishing every minute of this.

"Actually, I would like Mark to see it as well. I think he

should."

"Oh please!" I said "Don't make him feel badly about it or anything." I was quite sincere in expressing this, though I knew the whole house was horrified by what they had just seen.

"No. I want him to tell me whether he thinks tonight's treatment was adequate. He might decide it needs to be repeated a few times."

Clearly, I couldn't win, and made no reply. We understood each other.

5 JOHN MARK

Next morning found me lying face down on a sick bay table with a wet cloth covering my rear end. I had in fact reported soon after eight and Nurse Laurie MacIntosh had questioned me and already sent a young boy with a message to summon Mark. Mark brought Beaumont with him, and asked if he might come into the room also. Nurse Laurie raised her eyebrows, and consented. She waited until they would both be able to see clearly, and removed the cloth. I heard Mark take a quick breath. Then he composed himself and said:

"So this was the cane – but it was two weeks ago. And all this welt area was your slipper, eight wasn't it! It only just overlapped the old marks."

"Actually nine," I interrupted, rudely, "I was meant to be counting, but had to stop at about six. So I had just started to move as the last one landed. It must have missed where all the others hit, and made the old marks open up a bit. But no harm done!"

Even as I said this I thought, "That sounds stupid," but I let it stand. I was simply trying to cover for Beaumont, as I knew there had been no malice in his action. So I was relieved to hear Mark say:

"Thank you Beaumont. Well Done! ...you can go now; I want to talk to Lines for a minute."

As he said this, Nurse Laurie covered me up again and left to attend to some other boys. Mark moved quickly to the head of the bed, and squatted, facing me at eye level. He said nothing for a few seconds, and then began:

"Lines, all this is over now, and you can forget it – well, you know what I mean – I realize you will just never, never be able to forget it completely, but there is this meeting this afternoon at two o'clock – the whole afternoon is a washout as far as hockey is concerned. It would ruin all the pitches. There's been so much rain. So there is all the time in the world. It's in the Headmaster's study, and it is for the Head and me and you only – except I think the Major may be there." (Major – the Rev. N. Crowhurst) "The Headmaster depends on his advice in matters spiritual, I believe. Now, he's going to go over some things that are almost entirely good news for you, nothing to worry about at all. The only possible hitch I can see is that Dr. Gordon is going to be here soon, and Nurse Laurie thinks he may put you in the Sanitarium for a few days to let that heal. Anyway, I'll see you at mid-day, even if it is in the San." Mark rose and left. I had nothing to say. Events had been flowing fast, and it appeared that even some acceleration was impending.

Dr. Gordon was a large figure, late middle aged, and had seen service with His Majesty's forces on land. He came in after opening the door for Nurse Laurie, and sized up the condition immediately:

"Oh Yes! We used to see a lot of this. No! It's not infected, just inflamed. That's understandable, especially after last night's gentle aggravation.

"And these black strips are nearly ready to separate. They're just dead skin, that's why they're so black and leathery. Look, I'll show you." And with that he picked up some instrument (with the little "clank" and "tinkle" that one always hears as it is removed from the alcohol pan) and said:

"Lines, tell me if you feel this."

"Ow! Yes"

"This?"

"Yes."

"Now every time you feel a touch, you say, 'yes' loudly, right?"

I felt a few:

"Yes...Yes...Yes..."

"So there! You see Nurse. All the black pieces are quite dead. They're anesthetic. You can just cut them off – it won't hurt him at all – or not by your standard. Lines? What?"

"Perhaps I'll do it for you. Have some sponges ready. It'll bleed like anything of course, because it's so inflamed. But it'll soon stop. Always looks worse than it is."

So he did as he had said, but the procedure was not quite painless.

"There you are Nurse. Wonderful blood supply, healthy young man, won't get infected – well now - Iodine of course, then just zinc oxide paste, and dress it daily."

"Don't worry about the scars Lines, you won't be showing it off very often. And they shrink up beautifully at your age."

Mark came back about then, and Dr. Gordon said:

"That was the four-footer obviously. Excellent group – two inches I should think."

"Four feet long was it?" interjected Nurse Laurie. "Must have been at least half an inch thick to do that."

"Fifty-two inches actually," said Mark, "and five-eighths of an inch thick."

"Yes," said the good Doctor, as he washed his hands yet again. "I believe Marlborough have an old drawing and specification for it. Hardwood eh? Split, not sawn, like the old English pike."

"Ours is willow," explained Mark. "Actually that was the first time it was used since my predecessor got it out last summer. He wasn't using it properly anyway."

"Well it looks as if you're an expert. What do you do with a 303? You're on the team aren't you? A one inch group every time, I bet."

"I'd expect better than that sir, usually three-quarters. This term we won against Westminster and Charterhouse - drew with St. Paul's. The rematch is in the summer, but I will be away in uniform I hope." In fact Mark went to Cambridge for pre-clinical Medicine at the same time as I was in Mechanical Sciences. Neither of us was aware of the other during this period.

"Thank-you Nurse! Lines! – No sports for the rest of this term, understand? This needs rest. But it will heal well if you follow Nurse's orders."

Mark left with him and returned a few minutes later:

"So that clears you for the meeting this afternoon. That's good. Of course you realize I was reporting to the Head last night about what we had decided to do with you, and he has his own opinion on all that. He's still a little uneasy about the school discipline situation, because it's been worrying him for a long time. In fact, some time before the event of two weeks ago he told me to be on the lookout for some such situation, and possibly do something exemplary. It's obvious that you understand all that, and seemed to take our side from the start. Do you remember Stirzaker talking to you just after the beating?"

"The whole of every second of that experience is just implanted – for life, I should think. Yes. But I didn't understand what he was getting at. It was only later that I began to understand the 'exemplary' part of it. I mean it never struck me as unfair or anything."

"Well. That's not all." He went on carefully. "I know Beaumont and I give the impression that we are making light of it, but – not so. Beaumont was quite horrified when you started bleeding last night. Did you realize?"

"He couldn't hide it. Actually I think I helped him a little. He really fell for the Ilkley Moor bit. But of course he had to have the last word. I really never thought I would be able to rise to it like that."

"Peter saw and heard it all. He left the dormitory much better – tells me it was just as if you two had rehearsed it."

"Well, you know Beaumont. If it had been you or Peter in his place I wouldn't have dared to say all the things I did."

"I'm glad to hear that," said Mark. "I must say I had to go and look at the East House dormitory floor this morning. Your bed is easy to identify. I suppose they'll wash it off in the Easter holiday…"

"But do you know why I came straight round to the head of the bed this morning after dismissing Beaumont?

Well, I felt a bit sick. I had no idea that had happened. And as Dr. Gordon left he said quietly to me: 'You'll have to put that thing away, you know. Just use a Corporal's cane or something, and you could always give them a few more – eight or ten or a dozen if they need it.' So I don't think Stirzaker will use it at all."

Mark was actually letting out the news that Peter would succeed him next term. I didn't pick him up on this.

"Well, he couldn't do it as well as you can anyway. I doubt if anyone could."

Mark nodded agreement and went on:

"I had to tell you that. But I feel better about it now. You do seem quite amazingly generous – perhaps I mean forgiving."

This annoyed me a little – shouldn't have done. But I found myself saying:

"Just forget about that, and do brace up a bit too. You did your duty, and very well – nothing to forgive. We shook hands two weeks ago, remember? Actually I only just remember. My knees were giving way and if Peter hadn't held onto me I'd have fallen flat. But forget it."

"No!" Mark shook his head. "Most of us who were there will in fact not forget it – ever. See you at two o'clock."

He left quickly. I believe that short rebuke was what he needed at the time. He had taken it graciously.

6 HEADMASTER

The Headmaster's house stood alone on the West side, separated from the school by the Speech Hall. Walking past the front of the school was prohibited except for school prefects, although we ran squads there during House P.T. periods on some mornings. At five minutes to two I was walking briskly along the lower level corridor towards the school's West end exit when John Mark came running down the stairs. He greeted me happily:

"Oh, good! As I was telling you, all good news except for one little item you might find surprising. Amazing man! We met for such a short time last night, and he didn't waste a word – yet managed to teach me some Church history. He understands what a help you've been in all this, so that we've been able to concentrate on the school as a whole, and use you for the wider purpose."

Mark laughed a little as he said this. I did not know what he meant, and was careful not to ask.

Although he had tried to reassure me about the Head's intentions, I was still approaching the interview in trepidation. I said:

"Well at this stage I have no idea what else he has in mind, and the pain of the first beating keeps coming back. It's there now just from thinking about it. So, I can't laugh much at the moment, even if you can."

He laughed again at this, and then said:

"So, you won't forget it, will you? Poor Peter! He's had a hard time, you know – about you I mean."

This conversation had to stop as we approached the door. The maid answered the ring, and motioned us into the large study. Each time I saw it the size seemed to diminish – such is the effect of rapid physical growth. On the first day of my first term I had been here with my parents and since then only once about two years later to discuss the matter of the Royal Corps of Naval Constructors.

The Rev. D.G. Loveday taught classics to Group One of the sixth form, and took some part in five A Greek Testament and Latin. Every day he had the whole of the sixth in Divinity. Every few weeks he would post the title of a sixth form essay, and two of these recent titles had been:

"Specialization is the Bane of Education."
And "The Future of the Public Schools."

My essays had pointed out how education would change radically after the war, necessitating a higher level of compulsory science. (He had no science himself and could not drive a car.) I well understood this was not calculated to endear me to him, and earned myself a gamma for each. They were probably bad essays anyway. But my points were taken.

Major (the Rev. N.) Crowhurst was in the room, still standing, as the Head came in. He removed his mortarboard and sat down, pointing Mark and me to the opposite side of the large table. The Second Master sat beside him.

The Head started by asking me:
"When is your qualifying exam Lines?"

"Shortly after Easter Sir, I have to go up to Cambridge for it."

"This is a stiff exam, you know. It's usually taken late in the first year or early in the second. No one has taken it from here before. Do you think you have a chance of passing it? If you do it will be in the 'Cranleighan', of course."

"Oh yes Sir. I believe I'll pass it. It will be good to have it behind me after the war, - when I come back, I mean."

"Yes, I've been told you're trying to join the Fleet Air Arm. Admirable, I'm sure. But you must realize you would have no trouble at all if you were to ask for deferment."

"Yes Sir. But I would miss out on the war. I just hope I haven't missed it already."

"I hope it will be over soon." He said, looking sad for just a few seconds. I glanced at Crowhurst. There was the same expression on his face. So many young men whom they had known and taught would not return.

"You know that the rate of aircrew loss in the Fleet Air Arm is very high. So we have to use the word 'if', not 'when' (Crowhurst was nodding in agreement) – If you return you will be in the Honours Course, and the rate of attrition there is high, too. After the first year Mays, half of the class will be relegated to the General Course, and likewise half of the remainder at the second year, leaving only twenty-five percent to take the Tripos. And of course there are no second chances. Of that twenty-five only about two are awarded first class, and most of the others are thirds. You need a first or an upper second for the Royal Corps of Naval Constructors. How do you feel about that?"

"I'll be going for a first, Sir," I said, without hesitation. In fact I amply fulfilled this in '47 with a College Prize and senior scholarship

He turned to Mark,

"Certainly we can reassure Nurse MacIntosh that this boy has come to no permanent harm. I'll talk to her again later today." There was a twinkle in his eye, as well as the slightly puckered cheeks that were all he could allow to betray a smile. He had bad teeth.

"Now," he said, "to the matters in hand. There is a notice on my board which I have only just posted, - although the decisions were taken some weeks ago – listing East House prefects. These now number five, namely Sutton, your contemporary Tait I.G., you Lines, Fairbarns, and Flynn. (There is a separate notice elevating Beaumont to the rank of school prefect-at-large.) So you are in the third spot, senior to Fairbarns."

Fairbarns had been chosen by Blackshaw to supersede me the previous term.

A pause here, as he allowed the information to go home.

"I see, sir."

"Good. Now, our excellent Senior Prefect has kept me well informed about the sequence of events during the past two weeks, as well as the support that he has had from his colleagues. And I have had comments from many – not just two – of the teaching staff, volunteering their glowing reports of the all-round improvements in behavior, - politeness, attentiveness and so on, - all of which are bound to result in happier classes and teachers and in improvements in academic progress at all levels. I have commended Mark on the alacrity – derivation of that word, Lines?"

"Alacer, swift." I said

"Alacritas – promptness, better. But it also means joy, happiness. So – on the immediate, decisive action taken after the first deplorable incident. But also on the remarkable moderation and clemency with which he and his colleagues – and the East House prefects I understand – met your second, unfortunate challenge – I don't think that is too strong a term to use. And I take it as an indication of the confidence that remains in the effects, upon the school as a whole, of the first, exemplary punishment. I hope, but feel far from certain, that Mark's confidence is not misplaced. If he and his colleagues prove to be right, then this will be over now, Lines, and well taken by you, so far I believe. – So it is almost over – not quite – we'll return to that later."

I did not know what he meant (he must have intended this) or how much he had been told about the previous night's acid intercourse with Beaumont. But I saw his eyebrows raised at me with a question unframed and answered firmly:-

"Yes, Sir."

"Good! So, now to the second detail: - I have received in the post a remarkable letter from the Father of A.J. Lyne. You call him, 'Little A.J.', I believe, and he talks of you as 'Big A.J.'".

I began smiling.

"Yes Sir. We hardly knew each other until a few days ago."

"I won't read the letter. It might make you swollen-headed. But clearly you have been a great help to this child at a critical time in his school life. One of the things he told his Father was that you seemed to be the only kind hearted person here. – I'm sure you realize there are others Lines – for instance you are now under the care of Nurse MacIntosh, and you must appreciate her tender care for you."

"Oh, certainly, Sir. I do."

"Lines, this work with Little A.J. – seems to have been of a pastoral, even fatherly nature. And it was provided while you were still under some physical suffering yourself, was it not?"

I thought for a few moments, (the pain was back again) then said:

"Perhaps that had some kind of enabling effect. Actually he helped me a lot, too."

He and Crowhurst looked at each other. Crowhurst was beaming, but said nothing.

"Lines, are you quite sure you are called to Naval Architecture?"

"I wouldn't have expressed it that way Sir. But I want to do it."

"War and other experiences are bound to press in upon you. Do keep an open mind."

He was nodding to himself. I had to say again:-
"Yes, Sir."

"Now, to the last point. In our studies of Church history we did not go into much detail about the monastic institutions. But in the twelfth century and later, a few had an interesting feature in their rule. This was sometimes referred to as 'Compassion'- derivation, Lines?'

"Con-together, becomes com. before the P, and patior, I suffer, quasi-passive, pp. passus – 'sub Pontio Pilato passus est, et sepultus.'- so suffering together – used now of sympathy, mercy…"

"Indeed, yes. Your first interpretation gives the way it was understood, 'suffering together.' – I'm surprised that you seem to have some knowledge of the Nicene Creed in Latin."

-Each novice had one particular Brother, established in the Order, who was responsible for that initiate's progress – as his tutor, advisor, supervisor, who would devote much of his time and energy to the spiritual well being of his charge. Now if at any time or for any reason the Novice were found to be in need of some correction or penalty, then some penalty would fall upon his tutor also." (This slowly and with emphasis).

I was feeling uneasy already, and conjured up mental pictures of the Monks filing past the kneeling pair, giving equal and alternate lashes to repentant Novice and praying Friar. They probably did it in Chapel – had to be a Holy whipping – Ah Well! – lashes, a long cane - eight hundred years of progress…

"So, I have straightly charged Mark, and this will be transmitted to every Housemaster and school prefect, that if there be found any breach of discipline worthy of such punishment, then precisely the same will fall upon you. You must, Lines, understand the reasons for this. But I will repeat them. You have become an exemplar to many and if we are wrong in our assessment of the current situation, much blame for any changes for the worse must be seen to fall upon yourself; and you will share in any penalty resulting. This edict of compassion will remain in force for the remainder of this season of Lent – we break up in two and a half weeks' time, Thursday in Holy Week.

Now I realize, Lines, that you are not confirmed or even baptized. But it is very evident that you are not an unbeliever,

- from you behavior during the last two weeks, in several respects. So now you have two good reasons to enhance the intensity of any prayer life you may have. First, you have increased responsibility, with the duties required of a house prefect. Second, you now find yourself in some danger." He raised his eyebrows and nodded. "It will help you to pray not only for yourself but also for any potential miscreants in the school. Am I right thinking that you will give some diligence to these things?"

"Oh, yes Sir, I believe so."

"Very good and thank you both. We shall be praying as well, you understand."

"Thank you, Sir." We both said.

"That will be all. It is quite a lot to take in, isn't it Lines? God bless you."

"Amen! God bless you both." Crowhurst beamed again as he said this.

The Headmaster rose, stiffly, donned his mortarboard and strode out, bending slightly forward as usual, trailing his long gown and M.A. hood as he did so. We all stood as he did.

Crowhurst shook hands warmly with us both: -

"So, we're losing you at the end of this term Mark. You seem to be ending your career on a high note. Your handling of this situation has been superb, so far."

"Thank you Sir. I'm sure there will be a worthy successor."

In fact he had already advised that Peter Stirzaker should follow. I saw my own House Captain as the obvious choice.

As we left, Mark said:
"So! – Unbutton your coat."

The three button coat of the school uniform was worn with the centre button, only and always, fastened – except that house and school prefects were allowed to go about with the coat open – and always did so. I opened my coat. It felt strange, but good. We spent a long time walking back, rehearsing details of the Head's discourse. He had fitted in so many things in a short time that I was finding difficulty calling some of them to mind. But Mark had heard the basic details the previous evening, and it was evident to him that the decision to elevate me to house prefect status had been made long ago, probably about halfway through the term, and had taken Blackshaw by surprise. The Headmaster had stood by this, or rather felt it so much the more justified, after my response in the first event and by the good effect on morale in the school. He seemed to regard the threat of further punishment as complementary to what he thought was a trivial treatment the previous night.

Mark was saying:
"So although it's meant to be over, as far as you are concerned it is certainly not. I've really never seen him so emphatic about a thing. He had told me about it last night. That's what I meant about Church history. But this time he was looking right at me as he drove it home. So if anything happens, you may not even have time to find out why.

It'll just be a case of 'stick first, talk after." This expression was not Mark's original, but was known as one of Mr. Collinson's favourite dicta. In fact, during the following term, when Peter Stirzaker had become Senior Prefect, it was applied with just too much haste. On this occasion a few members of the Air Training Corps cut P.T. to practice their Morse code. This was a serious offence, and I overheard Peter discussing it with Collinson who said:

"Certainly Stirzaker! Stick them all, pretty firmly, will you?"

Evidently Peter left the action to Collinson himself who called them up and immediately told them their fate. Hicks Primus, a promising athlete in Collinson's House, One North, piped up.

"Well Sir, I for one refuse to be beaten…"

Collinson brooked no such gainsaying and interrupted:

"I see, Right! You first Hicks…Stick first, talk after. Wait outside, the rest of you."

Understandably, Hicks did not feel inclined to 'talk after', especially while his friends were waiting. But in the dormitory that night the House Captain told Collinson that Hicks was on the N.T.C. list ('not to change for games') for some minor malady so that he had been right to be absent from P.T. and his punishment had been undeserved apart from his rudeness of expression. Collinson at once apologized in front of the whole house, and Hicks and he happily shook hands again. Hicks said:

"I'm sorry I was so rude to you, Sir?" The situation was defused as the usual comments were heard:

"Hope it hurt anyway, Hicks" and "Many Happy Returns!" You'll always deserve it", etc.
One of the House Prefects said to Collinson:

"I'm sure we shouldn't worry, Sir, he must have earned

that beating somehow!"

Collinson had to add:

"And Hicks! Please don't start thinking you can bank that beating against the next offense. We'll just have to take that as it comes."

Mark went on:
"And it may be me or any of the school prefects or Housemasters. I think he intends to post this 'Edict of Compassion.' as he calls it, in the Common Room, so that none of them have to do any thinking about it. He doesn't want anyone's judgment about what should be done to any other boy to be clouded by worries about what happens to you at the same time. It just has to happen – a detail that is not their concern. All they have to do is send for you and do it. O.K.? I mean, do you understand?"

"What a funny...! Well, I suppose I do understand. And it may come to nothing anyway, so long as they behave themselves. But can you really expect Jake or Blackshaw to understand what is meant by an 'Edict of Compassion'?"

Mark was shaking his head. But he had to refute this expression of disrespect:

"Of course they will understand, even if they don't explain it so well as the Head".

I said," They might have a little difficulty. You will put their minds at rest won't you?"

Mark did not see the joke, a sarcasm. He remained serious.

We stopped walking, and stayed outside the West end, to

talk this over. He looked at me and held out a hand saying slowly,

"I can't think how you manage to say things like that. I just thank God that it's you and not anyone else."

I did not follow this up, but of course took his hand. He went on: -

"…And I should thank you for the way you spoke to me in the Sick Bay this morning." The discussion was becoming heavy again.

"About Peter," I said "-you told me he'd been having a bad time. Is he O.K. now? I know he had some kind of 'flu."

"Oh! – He'll be alright now, except if he has to call in one of his own East House boys for some detail."

I said: -

"I bet he'll know just what to do. He'll think about it for one and a half seconds, then there'll be a click somewhere inside, as he thinks 'this needs four – But since Lines gets it too.' He'll say, 'Right, go and get Lines here and tell him to wait outside. You'll have six each when you come back. Be quick, both of you."

Mark was nodding heartily, and laughing, "Yes, that's exactly what he'll do."

I went on, to press him about Peter.

"But now tell me honestly, did he let himself down last night – I mean at your meeting before supper?"

"No, not in the least, I was amazed how he and your

choir partner Nichols were talking. It was in fact my decision to change from the first idea – of another eight with the cane – to just the slipper instead. Even Nichols went along with it in the end. Of course your friendship with Stirzaker and Nichols has complicated this whole two weeks. But no one has let that temper any of the actions taken. We've all been really impressed by Peter's behavior all the way, just impeccable."

Mark looked up and saw me wiping my eyes. Finally, he had seen me shed a tear or two.

"I'm sorry." I said. "It has been quite a strain. Nobody could forget that pain. Maybe you've no idea. Nor had Peter. Some of the pain keeps coming back – like just now while the Head was talking. Maybe the nightmares will stop if you put that four foot cane away. And I'm so relieved about Peter. Fine chap! But you know that already….

Actually, I'm pretty sure Peter won't have any trouble, although it's the end of term. They're all duly terrified, to judge from the comments I heard as I walked into the bathroom to collect my pants this morning. They had been drying out overnight. But none of those comments was rude or disrespectful. I was really impressed. They had no idea that I was going to be promoted. Neither did I."

"Oh yes! Another thing…" He said. "Just the other day some of us were looking at records, and we realized how incomplete they are. Each of us could call to mind several beatings that are just not recorded at all – for instance, one that I took from Collinson about two years ago. Each House can have anything from two to as many as fifteen in one term. Big variations, East and West Houses have the least. One North is far the worst - Two North second. There are two peak periods – one round about halfway to two-thirds way through the term; then the biggest peak in the last two weeks, when all the badness comes out. Somehow the bad ones bunch up and make each other worse. So at the average of about four per house per term, as many as half are in the last two weeks. Now, work it out. Two per house, six houses, equals twelve to come during the next two weeks. One of the best was last term, just three. And one of the worst was the term before, July '43, when there were fifteen. Lent term is usually the best. So under this Edict your chances of getting away with nothing are about nil, unless my expectations are bang on target. If not, you could have one to three or more surprises, anytime out of the blue. I'm sure the Head has no idea the figures are so high. But obviously he would hear no dissenting opinion. – Crowhurst was silent, wasn't he? But that makes it look pretty harsh. I just hope, for your sake, that nothing happens to disturb our peace." He was sincere, but was showing much more sympathy towards me than his rank should have allowed.

I maintained a wonderful respect for Mark. His duty was always paramount to him, and he fulfilled it exactly as the Headmaster and Crowhurst expected. After Nurse MacIntosh had expressed her feelings, (to an extent that I never knew at any time) and his first reaction at the sight of the damage he had caused he had reason to feel at least uneasy. But I had to admire the way he was able to keep his guard up, and I felt happy for him at the Head's reassurance that I had come to no permanent harm, and again as the Major congratulated him on the whole issue without so much as a glance in my direction. But he was now also a friend, and I was pleased to be able to help him, even though I knew that we might find ourselves again at opposite ends of the stick. He would hate it. But he would do it and not allow so much as a flicker of facial expression to betray his own feelings. There would follow the simple handshake of perfect understanding and again, no reproach.

This had been an extraordinary conversation, since I had not dreamt, only two weeks before, of ever being able to address him in familiar terms. Yet the result of these processes of discipline was not to drive us apart but rather to enable each to understand the other.

So, our discussion evolved. Mark and I were both looking serious as we went up and into the front entrance. This was a marble-floored hallway between the vestry and a cloister leading to the chapel. Mark went ahead, quickly. I hung back; then on impulse, turned right, to go into the Chapel. I walked slowly and quietly towards my usual place at the back of the North side choir stalls. As I passed across the aisle and looked at the Altar, I saw two men in black gowns on their knees, silent. They were Loveday and Crowhurst.

I found myself kneeling, weeping, and feeling alone. This was the catharsis I needed. From time to time I heard low voices, but did not try to make out what was said. I soon felt relieved, not realizing that I had not been alone at all. I did not appreciate this until a few years later. But the picture of those two great men, kneeling together with heads bowed at the Altar remains clearly in mind. They were still there when I left. It was known that they each spent long periods in the Chapel and I began to understand that they must have been in prayer for unknown hours before the meeting that had just taken place, and that they too must feel relief, having finally unloaded so concisely the results of these decisions upon Mark and me who now carried the onus of seeing them put into effect.

1. Inside the quad looking South. Formerly a tarmac covered parade ground with cloisters open to the weather. All top floor windows belonged to East House dormitory which covers the library and reading room.

2. Original building from the Southeast.

3. Chapel and East entrance to old buildings.

4. Speech Hall and new building.

5. Just inside the main entrance looking North to quad. Marble hallway between reading room to left and library room to right.

6. Front of a girls' house new in the 1970's.

ALFRED J. LINES

7 THE QUIET TIME AND NICHOLS

The remaining few weeks of the Lent term passed happily. In East House, we agreed that there would be no need for me to settle into the number two East study next door 'til the following term, as all my books were well organized in the one I was already using. Flynn moved in immediately from the Houseroom lockers, which were always too small. Duties started the following day, when Tait asked me to take call-over for him, as he was suddenly wanted with others on the shooting team, for some extra practice detail. Call-over bell was at four fifteen when everyone had to be in his houseroom, prefects included, for a roll call. All stood in line, easy, and at the bell snapped to "at ease". As each boy's name was called, he would answer: - "Sum" an abbreviation of 'Adsum'. Count complete, the prefect would report the fact to the school prefect for the week at the main bell, then return to the houseroom and ask: "Changing room?" Whereupon the boy responsible would reply, "Changing room, tidy," or if necessary hand a list of "found" details or untidy lockers to the prefect, and those named would need some trivial penalty. When I was a new boy this was usually to learn by rote about a dozen lines of whatever Shakespeare play was being studied by fifth form English classes. But this slowly gave way to the much simpler system of being listed for the slipper the same night.

This day I had the reply: "Changing room tidy", and simply awaited the second bell, which was in effect a "dismiss" or "stand down". All were free to go into Hall for a cup of tea and a biscuit or bun. The same had happened to Beaumont, newly a school Prefect, who was acting at the bell for another member of the shooting team.

I found the extra time, from not being involved in hockey practices or the house runs that had to suffice for exercise when the fields were too wet, to be most valuable in clearing up some maths problems especially as I could ask our excellent teacher – Bob Hall - to help me out when I was stuck.

And at last I began to heal. The work of Dr. Gordon proved to be the turning point, and at each day's Sick Bay procedure Nurse Laurie or her associate seemed to have less mess on the old dressings. After about two weeks she said the biggest hole was filing up, and all it would need then was to grow some new pink skin over the top. "So by next term it should be healed over."

"Like new, you mean?" I asked.

"Well, yes. Like new but not like it was. And the other two little lines will stay there as well. So just you behave yourself and don't get into trouble again, or all our work will be spoiled in no time."

"That's just it. – It's not up to me entirely. I suppose you know about that."

"Well, yes. Mark was telling us both. He thinks it's so unfair – at least he dare not say that, but he can't help showing it. He's quite worried about you. It's obvious what he thinks inside. It must be just the Headmaster's idea. I don't understand him sometimes."

"That's right," I said, "Nobody does. He is so learned, and no one would dare to cross him – certainly not on a matter of discipline, least of all his Senior Prefect. I think there is a notice up in the Masters' Common Room as well."

The two nurses had noticed an all round improvement in

behavior – better manners from all the boys, consistently. Nurse Laurie said she thought the boys were even more considerate of each other. After talking it over we came to the conclusion that it was not just that they were terrified by the tale of what had happened to me, but the next thing that followed was the discovery that Mr. Wicks, by far the oldest teacher, was certainly worth listening to, and was enjoying his teaching. Further, that the only female teacher on staff was also a really good person, deserving of all the support and respect that boys can provide.

Mark became more friendly, and looked genuinely happy in the last few days of term, saying that I was looking –"better at last. You haven't looked fit for weeks you know. That was another thing that was worrying Peter."

I was able to tell him that at last I was not having nightmares, although sometimes pain would wake me up at night and I would find myself sweating and frightened again. We enjoyed congratulating each other on the behavior of the school in general.

In fact, John Mark was never a close friend. The difference in rank was too great, and his interests were almost entirely athletic, whereas my performance in sport was dismal.

Peter Stirzaker and I were less often together in those last few weeks of Lent. We were both studying hard. We still sat together in the Head's Divinity, and in English classes.

English was compulsory at all levels. Our teacher was somewhat of an innovator. For instance, he had us compare three different Old Latin versions of Isaiah LX 1-3 with the Vulgate, St. Jerome's translation, (not from the Septuagint which St. Paul used but from the Massoretic Hebrew) and then with some English versions, including the Bishops', the Breeches, and the newer Authorized of 1611. He was not interested in accuracy of translation, but in the flow of the prose, the cadences when read aloud, the likely ease of memorization, and musicality – all qualities that we had not even thought of seeking in O.T. Scriptures. He was himself an excellent reader, and the whole school was attentive when he approached the Lectern. He sung tenor parts in the Choir.

Readings by the Head were also memorable, since he did not glance down at the Bible, but rather declared the Scripture reading – knowing it perfectly, - while he gazed straight forward upon the Altar.

The V-1 period was beginning, and we became used to the sound of their noisy "pop-pop-pop" engines. It was a brilliant invention. The flying bomb was boosted, for take-off, by a simple rocket, and then at a high sub-sonic speed its propulsion was self-sustaining. The air intake had shutters allowing entry of air, for combustion, from the front. Fuel was sprayed in and the mixture, ignited I believe by sparks, burned rapidly, closing the shutters at the front, and exhausting with great force through a nozzle at the back. Voila! Thrust from what became known as the "pulse-jet" principle. Flight continued with a straight course and fixed altitude, gyro controlled, until fuel exhaustion. Then the engine stopped and after some seconds of silence there was an explosion. Here, more German brilliance. The nose had a nine-foot-long projection, and at impact the one-ton charge was all above ground level. This made no crater, but in London, a crowded conurbation thirty miles and more in diameter, a whole terrace or block of brick houses could be razed.

Only head on approach could intercept these weapons, as their speed was greater than any propeller-driven fighter could attain. It was better to shoot them down over the countryside of Kent, Sussex, or Surrey than over London. But better still was to destroy them over the English Channel.

The clever Germans had them flying below radar detection level.

There were a few surprises. During the next, or summer term, on one very hot night, when the platoon of Home Guard with the duty of anti-paratrooper patrolling round the village, were lying on straw palliasses with heads outside the tent talking, looking up at the stars and the V'1's far and near, one passed directly overhead, and as it did so, stopped.

Conversation ceased. This particular bomb, like no other we had heard of, instead of coming down to a point a quarter of a mile ahead of it's fuel cut-off point, managed to turn to one side, and detonated outside the village, hurting no one. But the platoon had to spend the rest of the night sweeping up glass and debris, which had been sucked out of windows into the main street. Damage was minimized by the fact that adhesive tape of various kinds had been in place over almost all the glass doors and windows. So that was our closest call with flying bombs – just a deafening explosion that lit up the night for a second or so. The Germans were always full of stupid propaganda about how frightened they thought we were. In fact we were – I hate to admit it – enjoying the war more than ever, realizing that it would soon be finished.

End of term always brought some exuberance. The official break up day was Thursday in Holy Week. Serious classes ended on the previous Friday, and periods on the Monday and Tuesday were less intense. The Headmaster's Divinity classes were unchanged as were some of the others, on the first three days of the last week. Our Group Four physics, run by the Second Chaplain, was a delight and Bob Hall's maths I was still most earnest about. Peter was serious with his studies up to the last minute also. We were expecting some light-hearted seven-a-side hockey. But rain frustrated almost all of this and for exercise most of the houses went on runs.

The shortest run was the Short Junior. The route left the country road about a mile away, to cross a few fields, then to the North end of a long gentle down slope at Healey's field, finally reaching a road again about half a mile from the school. Total distance was about two and a half miles. The Long Junior was nearer to four miles, starting and finishing the same way, but going through some beautiful beech forest. It included a few steep hills. Most senior boys enjoyed it more and took it by choice. But to the Juniors it was too much like hard work and not so well appreciated.

Only East House had the Venner Run. This covered about a mile further still, along a path over Smithfield Common, with a total rise of about four hundred feet. I had been forbidden, by the Doctor, to do this when I first came to the school. But I had started to ignore all advice in 1943 and seemed to come to no harm.

This year, about half way through Lent term, we had a wet run. But most of us enjoyed it. Stirzaker and Fairbarns were easily faster than the rest. I was about average for age. Blackshaw was at the finish and seemed surprised that I was anywhere near up to even that pace.

Most of the houses were quiet until in the last week we heard that One and Four South had had a common-consent houseroom slippering of one of their most bratty juniors. East House never did these.

On the Wednesday just after lunch, six of the One North boys from the Middles went wild. They hauled in, from the main corridor into their changing room, a few of the passing small boys that happened to look easy prey, and in a few minutes had stripped them, daubed them with black shoe polish and thrown their clothes out of the windows onto the ground on the North side of the school. Then they chased their naked victims out into the main corridor. They were hoping that they would be so quick about it all that they would get away with the whole thing.

They very nearly succeeded, as this was soon after lunch and changing for games was not allowed till two o'clock. But their own Housemaster, Collinson, caught sight of the last of the naked boys running into his own changing room and at once guessed, quite correctly, that the culprits must be boys from his own house. He ran straight to One North changing room in time to find them laughing as they put away their tins of shoe polish.

Collinson was known for wasting no time with these things, and simply said:

"Right, how many of you are there? – I see, six?" Is there anyone hiding in the shower room?" He went round to check for himself, although hiding was impossible – there were no doors inside any changing room complex.

"So, you'd better all have a pee first. Then go up to the bathroom. You'll all get six; I'll see you there immediately. And – Spence – go and tell Lines I want him too, now. He'll be in his study."

Spence knocked on my door and came in looking sheepish. He said;

"Mr. Collinson wants you in One North bathroom straight away. He's got six of us, and he says he's going to give us six each."

I said:

"So, you must deserve it. What's it all about?" I had jumped up as soon as he mentioned One North bathroom and went straight to the nearest place to pee as well. On the way, Spence told me the whole short story. He seemed contrite already, and started apologizing to me for the fact that I had to be treated in the same way.

We caught up to Collinson just as he arrived at the bathroom door. This was not like the nightmares at all. I felt absolutely on Collinson's side. As he turned, I said:

"Very well done, to catch them at it like that Sir! I'm sure this is richly deserved."

"Yes, Lines. It is. You understand you have a share in it, do you?"

"Oh yes Sir. That was made very clear to Mark and me, just a few weeks ago. In fact, this is the first breach of discipline in the whole school since then. Naturally, I hope it's the last."

"We'll just have to see, won't we? Wait outside. You'll be last. I'll have got my eye in better by then."

He called them in one at a time. To my surprise, not one of them was quite silent and there were several squeals. Each one had been told to wait outside afterwards. Finally I went in. He was quite cheerful, saying:

"So now for you Lines, after that little bit of practice. Bend down."

When he had finished, and I felt able to speak I turned to him and said as we shook hands,

"I'm sure they were all duly impressed Sir. But what was all that noise about?"

He shook his head, then:

"Tell me honestly, Lines. How does that compare with John Mark?"

"There's just no comparison, of course. Because that 'four foot', so called is in fact fifty-two inches – about twice the length of your corporal's cane – and much thicker. So – sorry to disappoint you Sir, but that whole beating is no where near as painful as his first stroke, even – Nothing like it!"

"I thought so. And he's nearly a foot taller than me, and much stronger. He took it round about five hundred degrees. You wouldn't have seen that. But he had been practicing that move. That's why he put you over the third bath. He told me about it."

"I had some idea. I heard him do a few paces 'dance' just before each hit. So, thank you for telling me Sir. Now I don't feel so bad about being white and wobbly afterwards. I need to go for a run now. I haven't done anything for a month. And thank you for missing Mark's damage completely."

I went straight out past his "One North Babies", calling them just this as I walked away. Collinson, close behind me, was quick with the handshakes, and saying, "You heard what he said. He's quite right of course. Now get out of my sight and behave yourselves."

I realized that I wasn't going to be able to concentrate on maths, especially as I was still at risk under the edict.

I walked carefully down the stairs, to find Nichols coming from Two North changing room, in white running shorts and T-shirt.

"Oh Lines! Do you feel like a short run?"

I said:

"I'm so unfit. I've done nothing for two weeks – Dr. Gordon's orders. But I'm sure it'll be O.K. now. You'll find me slow. But it's just what I need."

"No, I don't want to go fast either. I'll tell you about that."

Then as I went into East House changing room, he came in too. – School prefects had this open privilege.

"Can I have a look at your taps, pipes and things?"

"Do, certainly – we've just had some of the kids on them with rags and Brasso. They're beautiful."

I changed out quickly. Nichols carefully inspected the hot and cold water lines and the washbasins drains. Sure enough, they were gleaming. Some boys had been fidgeting on Chapel line when our backs were turned. I had heard it, spun round and caught them. So, during the morning break I had shown them how to use long strips of cloth and Brasso to bring up a high polish on all the old copper pipes and brass fittings, and then had them sitting on the floor, each with an assigned area to clean. They had sixteen sets for three boys. I did one, leaving five each, so that they had a standard to achieve. They rose to it cheerfully, finishing just as Nichols and I arrived.

We started the run quite slowly, heading for the confluence of the Long and Short Junior routes – going in the opposite of the usual direction. He was saying:

"I don't want to go far. This is just a kind of leg stretcher." Then he began to open up. He had put some of the Two

North boys on the same task as I had done in East, for similar, comparable trivial offences but had found that instead of really polishing, they had tried to take short cuts, rubbing the pipes with fine emery cloth, lengthwise, leaving the parts against the wall untouched. So he had told them, rightly, that this was a lazy attitude to it and sent them off round the Long Junior.

"Why don't you show them the East House pipes first? Then they'll see just how well it can be done if they try?"

He said:

"Good idea! But I have the impression this is a lazy crowd, and that in fact they've already decided to cut the run short and go round the Short Junior – probably walking. That's why I'm going this way. And if I'm right we should catch them at it as they come down Healey's Field."

I said:

"If they're thinking they won't come down Healey's at all. They'll cross the top and head for the place where the Long Junior comes out." Then I laughed. "I know what you're coming to. It's that if you turn out to be right you have to stick them all. So I have to be there. I bet that's it. Eh?"

"Yes." He said, "But I've thought quite a long way ahead. I was going to come and get you, and would have been up to your study if you hadn't been coming down just then. Also I had thought of the Healey's Field thing and as you probably know I can't see that far, whereas I'm sure you can. So you can be a real help, spotting for me from a distance."

"You've thought it all out in detail, haven't you?" I said, grinning broadly.

He was really quite a harmless person. I saw no reason to complicate things by telling him about the encounter with Collinson, although I was still hurting.

"Then there's another thing," he said, "well, actually two things. I'll tell you one of them now. You may or may not know that I've never been this end of a stick before. I've been your end, a few times, yes. But nobody looks round to watch it. And since I need a witness, I'm sure you could help."

I said:

"Well why not? But you can't go far wrong. You are going to use…"

I stopped myself;

"I should not be putting ideas into your head. So I should ask you carefully. Which stick are you going to use?"

He said:

"That's right. It ought to be in the interrogative. The answer is – the Corporal's cane. It's the shortest, so probably the easiest to use. And since they'll be – you'll be – in just these light shorts; it ought to be painful enough. Not really a serious offence. But a stick is absolutely standard for any P.T. or games-related thing."

"I'm sure it's not difficult." I said, "We used to watch our Headmaster at prep school, through his study window. He always used a Corporal's cane, steel tips, flexible. They never break. Main things is, don't stand too close, or behind him at all. Stand at the side, left foot forward, feet wide apart, and swing from the hips. Measure it, so that with your arm straight, at impact, the tip just hits the right side, and the left side gets the rest. Just like a tennis forehand. You're driving to the back of the court – horizontally. Wrist comes in last. Don't worry about it. You can't hurt him with that thing. That's not really what I mean – hurts like hell – you hope. But you don't do him any harm, and the bruises go away in two weeks, or three. Actually that means they will still be there when next term starts."

"Thanks. But maybe I'm wrong about this crowd. I certainly hope so for your sake."

Then he began laughing, after saying this.

"I think I know what you're laughing at. You'll put me down last, so that you'll have plenty of practice by that time. Perhaps I'm just fated to be a helpful person." I was laughing with him, although I was not able to be quite so happy about it.

We reached the bottom end of Healy's Field and waited until we began to despair of seeing them at all. At this rate, perhaps they were on the long route after all. No one could fault them for walking most of the way.

We had almost given up when I caught sight of five boys strolling along the other side of the wood towards the upper end of the field, all in white except for one pair of blue rugger shorts. We stayed still, barely concealed, as they crossed over the upper end. Then we trotted slowly along the road to meet them. It was up a gentle slope, a typical Surrey country road, sunken with high banks and a complete overhead cover of beech branches just beginning to bud.

The term 'sunken' is not quite true of course. These roads have been formed by centuries of use by coaches, carts, farm workers plodding to and from their fields, by herds and flocks driven along them, by horsemen in peace and various tribal wars, and doubtless marching Romans. Seasons of rain had deepened ruts. Parish workers must have dug, picked and shoveled the centres 'til the axles of carts and coaches could clear them. Finally the Macadam road builders came. Then last of all tar (Tar Macadam – hence the word 'Tarmac').

The boys hove in sight at last. I was able to recognize them, and as I did so called their names to Nichols. One had navy rugger shorts, the rest white.

"Bad luck, Lines." Said Nichols, as we turned and ran home with them.
By the time we reached the school, Nichols had told them what to do, and what to expect. We were to meet them in Two North bathroom immediately. He was careful to say:

"Have a pee first, that's all you have time for. Don't change at all."

I went straight to their bathroom and had a quick pee there. The others soon came too, and then Nichols with his short stick. While he, in turn, was shaking it out, I said:

"May I make a simple suggestion?"

"Yes, but what is it?"

"Just that one of them is a new boy, Effingham, and it might be kindest to start with him – I hope you don't mind me mentioning kindness at this point – and finish with Jenkins. He's the eldest by at least a year, and should know better. But you know all about that example thing, I'm sure."

We didn't laugh now, with all the boys there.

Nichols turned as he put it away.

"Right, all of you except Lines and you, Effingham, wait outside."

So, he motioned Effingham to the nearest bath, and said:

"Bend down. Lines is my witness."

He was just a little too close and I said:

"Further back, and swing as if you are going straight through. Don't swing your body towards him."

He moved back and did it perfectly. Be he wasn't doing his best. I knew how his Standing Orders expressed it. But I had to be careful not to advise him too strongly.

Effingham stood up stiffly and Nichols told him to ask one of the others in, and wait outside. As he went towards the door, I said:

"Can you think of anything in your Standing Orders that was missing there?"

"Yes," he said, "it reads – 'Each stroke shall be…'"

He didn't need to finish it, as I started nodding firmly. "Yes."

"But you're quite right. He's only thirteen."

He did the others progressively harder, then really laid into Jenkins. He had been placing all his shots accurately, right in the middle, below Collinson's favorite point of aim. I was of course delighted to see this, and after Jenkins I had to congratulate him, if only out of self-interest.

"That's all perfectly grouped and exactly the right place. I'll tell you why later." I said.

But then as Jenkins turned to go outside, Nichols said:

"Now Jenkins, you don't wait outside. You call the others back in."

This surprised me a little. Nichols explained it to us all.

"You must all know by now that the Headmaster decided, over two weeks ago, that Lines would have to share in any punishment of this kind for the remainder of this term. Now, nothing had happened to Lines until today and I can't help but think that the headmaster has been surprised by the continuance of good behavior throughout the school. Lines has been agreeably surprised as well. So were Mark and the rest of us – until today. That's right, isn't it Lines?"

"Certainly is." I said.

"So, now it's Lines' turn. And since he has been present, watching each of you being beaten, you will now all be present watching him have the same. – Fair's fair, Lines?"

I had to say:

"Yes, it is."

"Now another detail is this. I told you on the run Lines that I had two more things to explain. You will now hear the second of these.

You see, I decided that for this offence the appropriate number of strokes was four. But others are bound to say, 'Should have been six', and it would have been if his friend Lines hadn't been there. But we can't allow people to say that, can we Lines?"

I'm sure I coloured up, as I said:

"Quite right, I suppose we can't. And the corollary of all that is that there is also no reason why these boys should have six just because I'm here, so…"

I left him to finish it. It was obvious what was coming next. But he didn't take it up – just said:

"So, carry on. What happens now?"

I waited a few moments before filling in the details.

"So now the boys each having had four may have to watch me get more than that."

"Exactly, and this is a copy of my Standing Orders. It includes these words."

He read the complete sentence that I had started quoting.

"Who do you think wrote that Lines?"

He was holding the stick under his left arm as he handed me the loose-leaf notebook.

"I've no idea. But it's probably only a re-write of a re-write of a copy of something from the last century."

"Not that old. This one is signed by MacIntosh."
"That old bast…" I began to say.

Then I realized that Nichols was crossing himself. He had put the stick down. He was furious. MacIntosh had been Senior Prefect (and previously Two North House captain), when Nichols and I had been new boys three and a half years before. He was in fact a cousin to Nurse Laurie.

"No!" I said. "Is he dead?"

"Didn't you know? Crete I think it was, or North Africa. He had a D.S.O. or something by that time. But that didn't keep him alive did it?"

We both hung our heads. I was feeling deeply ashamed as I said:

"Dulce et decorum est"
"Pro patria mori". He joined in.

Then:
"Restat in pace." I said.

Nichols crossed himself again as we joined;
"Et lux aeterna luceat eo"

Except that he said:

"Eis."

"Eo." I corrected him.

We said it again, and Nichols crossed himself again as he stared at me, still angry, but calmer now.

"Do you realize that of the Senior Prefects from him to Mark, there's probably only one alive and he has a plaster cast on one leg?"

"No, I didn't...I shouldn't have said that." I said, "Do you think he'll forgive me?"

Nichols made no reply at first. Then he said slowly:

"Penance would help."

We were both looking down at the table, with the cane lying on it.

I was a long time answering while these words took their permanent place in my mind. The boys had heard all this and I turned to them as I said:

"Never, never dishonour the dead. They died for us. Remember! Yes, Nichols, I know what you mean. Now can I ask you a favour?"

"Not that you're in a position to. But what is it?"

"Well, these boys are not going to forget this. And I'm not going to be fit to explain it to them any time soon. So could you make quite sure they know what it's all about before you start? You know you are going to do the right thing. But they have to understand too. And they ought to be here – for your sake."

I just stood and waited while he talked to them kindly and respectfully about MacIntosh. Then he turned back to me and took both my hands with both of his. I had my back to the boys just then. As we clasped firmly, I said:

"Nichols, you're shaking. Don't! And don't worry."

"You're shaking too." He said, "And so you should be."
He was going to perform as expected. Then he said loudly:

"So it's eight Lines." I tried to make no response whatever apart from complying silently. I was in fact relieved that it was not more. Certainly the Headmaster or Crowhurst would have been angered by my outburst of a few minutes before.

Nichols did everything right. But I had to go straight to the bath taps without standing up, and douse myself with cold water. As I started to straighten up I heard him say:

"No! Sit down, or lie down, better. You're dead white."

I lay down for a few moments, writhing slowly, then rose to hands and knees saying:

"Sorry about that Nichols! That's twice I've done that now. Never used to. Not your fault. I must be holding my breath or something. It didn't happen this afternoon."

But I was soon over it, standing firmly – realizing I had just said, "this afternoon," in a moment of less than clear thinking. Then it was handshake time. The boys were obviously impressed and relieved by this little ceremony. Now they knew their House Captain better. Two of them were wiping their eyes. As they turned, I said:

"Me too please. I was coaching your House Captain – telling him how to make it hurt."

They were all happy to shake hands. I told them:

"If it's MacIntosh you want to cry about – go ahead. He won't mind."

As they left, Nichols called out to them:

"Finish those pipes after Call Over. Then we'll all have a look at East, if Lines lets us in. We'll see if you can do an even better job than they have."

I could not help thinking what perfect manners he had.

Then he turned to me saying: -

"Now you have to do some explaining to me. Do you remember, after Jenkins, something about the group?"

"Yes, I was smiling then for a completely selfish reason."

"Aha! Now I'm all ears. And what was that you let slip about 'this afternoon'?"

"I didn't realize I'd said that till it was too late. I thought you might just miss it. But..."

At this point I told him the story of the 'One North Babies' and how Collinson always grouped his at the top, a long way away from the small dressing that I still had on Mark's damage.

"I was delighted that all of yours were grouped close together, right in the middle, so that you would still miss Mark's work and miss Collinson's too."

"I saw that dressing through your gym shorts, and more clearly still when we were all a bit wet from the rain. So I knew I could miss it. That's why I didn't question you about it. If only I'd looked for myself I'd have seen Collinson's work. Actually I can see both his and mine now, through those shorts."

"Well, it's a good thing you didn't look too closely before. You had your own problems – I mean just with our friendship. I saw no reason to complicate things. You had a solution worked out already. That was before I made that dreadful remark that made you so angry. Then you solved that one too by cooling off as you talked to the boys. Before that, from the look on your face I didn't know whether to expect ten or twelve – I was just frightened. Then I was so relieved when you said 'eight'. I have to thank you for that – honestly! I bet you'll never hear that said to you again. And yes, I was shaking. That's another precedent, Nichols – I mean shaking hands like that before you did it. I hope it helped you like it did me. Don't ever reproach yourself. It's over."

We separated. I went to shower off and change back. There was no one else in the East House showers. I was even able to check out the effects in the changing room mirror, by climbing on to the lockers opposite. No harm beyond the expected red and black welts. This would not bleed or scar at all. Later that day there was a little oozing, but it all dried up leaving no remnant. The new skin was perfect and undisturbed; only one small patch remained. Nurse Laurie had discharged me that morning with some dressing materials, saying she wanted to check it quickly next morning, as well as at the beginning of the next term. That would be nearly three weeks later.

After Call Over I was still suffering from – not just pain, - but a sense of anticlimax. And I had to pull myself up sharply to remember that, pain or no, that dreadful Edict was still in force. I went up to the study to put away the papers I had left out before Spence had called me, then realized I wasn't going to be able to concentrate anyway. I met Nichols as I walked slowly towards the top of the staircase.

"Where are you going?" he asked.

"I thought I'd just go into the Chapel." I said: "Why do you ask?"

He turned round and didn't say a word. We walked slowly together. On the way past Two North changing room Nichols opened the door. His boys were sitting on the floor and chatting as they worked away with their strips of cloth and a Brasso Pot. Nichols began to look less unhappy.

"So you helped them a lot." I said.

He needed encouragement. Neither of us could say much at first. We had done most of the talking that afternoon but feelings had been running high, and action had been intense for us all. While walking along the cloister he began to weep a little and started to say: -

"What have I done, Alfred? Those boys looked bad too. They weren't crying about MacIntosh."

"I know." I said, "But I believe they needed a let-out just then. I was feeling sorry for them. They'll remember this for the rest of their days."

At last he had decided to be a friend, probably as close as Ian Tait or Peter. I had to put an arm on his shoulder.

"I felt terrible when you went so white, just horrible. It wasn't so bad when Mark had done it. Even then, Passmore and Janes were turning away as Stirzaker held on to you. Then two weeks later I wanted Mark to go ahead and do eight with a stick and then pour cold water on you to stop you fainting, just to make sure you didn't miss the pain. That's terrible."

"Never mind, it didn't happen. And by the way, you've put on twenty-eight shots today. And Collison did forty-two without batting an eyelid. Actually you're much better at it than he is. Today you did everything you should have done as far as I can see. And what do you think MacIntosh was doing when he was killed? Just his duty. So if we are going to honour the dead we can start by doing that. Nothing more required. Nothing less will do. So can't we just go, thank God, and simply carry on. Then next time – just do our duty again – whatever it is. Like taking Hall or Call Over or…"

So, we reached our places, next to each other in the back row of the Choir stalls, - two grown men, not ashamed to weep…

Dennis, or Nichols D.C., as he was known, was an interesting person. He was quietly sure of his faith, having grown up through the established Anglican path of Infant Baptism, Catechism and Confirmation. He seemed to not question any of the great Doctrines, and had a clear understanding of sin, repentance, forgiveness, and of course redemption. But he seldom spoke of these things. He did not know just how much power had gone into those three short words he had been given to speak, when I was feeling despair and shame.

We left after about ten minutes of silence. He had been in prayer, while I had been questioning again and again to myself:

"Why did I come in here? I don't really believe all this, do I?"

As we walked slowly out stopping every few yards, I was expressing some of these things to him. He was saying: -

"No! You can't possibly tell me you're not a believer, and believe what you're saying. Just look at all the things going on around you. You may never understand what a help you've been to me today and to Peter two weeks ago. Even John Mark has changed a bit. Then there was that kid, Little A.J. And the whole tone of the school sharpened up a month ago, and hasn't altered. You must have seen the respect yourself."

"I have been feeling it actually. It's surprising. But, about MacIntosh…"

He cut me off.

"I'm absolutely sure he would forgive you – for a whole lot of reasons. There's the way you felt so ashamed about it, and said so – in effect asked him to forgive you. Do you remember that?"

He reminded me. He had been noting, mentally, all these things that pertained to the health of my soul, even when he was so angry, and he went on to a stumbling block that I was going to meet again and again.

"Do you know what the most difficult part is when it comes to forgiving? It's not forgiving other people – you are doing that all the time. It's actually accepting it when you need it yourself, and it's there for the taking."
He was talking to me for a long time. And these are just some of the gems that I carried with me and appreciated better as the years passed.

I was back in my study when there was a knock at about five thirty.

"Come."

Mark came in, smiling. I stood at once, and waited.

"Guess what! The Major wants us both down at his house. He's just walking down there now. So we can catch him up. He was obviously pleased about something."

So we walked down there briskly.

"You've had quite a day, haven't you? Dennis was talking to the Major about it. So he knows all the details. I didn't really know Dennis before. But you two have suddenly come to know each other much better – with mutual benefit, if I understand."

"I'm sure you do understand. But do you know, we've been sitting next to each other in Chapel and been to choir practices together for nigh on two years, and have hardly spoken to each other closely 'til the last few weeks, especially today.

Do you remember the Headmaster asking me if I was called into Naval Architecture? Just the question shot me down. But honestly Dennis should be in the church. Do you know him well?"

"I suppose not. But from his attitude at a certain meeting we had…"

"He told me about that – he was quite ashamed of it. I'm sure he's recovered from that now. Yes. He had a terrible sense of guilt – poor guy! But that's all a bad dream – clean gone – if you can understand that. That's what I mean about the church. He's had some experiences, and learned from them. He wants to do Law, I believe."

Mark didn't say much. Crowhurst was only just ahead of us. He welcomed us into his study, explaining that the Headmaster was unwell (he had migraines), and had deputed all his functions since the previous day.

"First, Lines. Mark is aware of the events of today. Concerning the first of these – not so much a breach of discipline as an outburst of rebellion from some boys whom Mr. Collison had been watching and privately assessing for some months. He tells me he was surprised that they had restrained themselves this long and had been expecting to catch them at just such a prank as this. He was in fact speaking favourably of your attitude from start to finish. He didn't discuss any of this with you, did he?"

"I'm sure it wasn't necessary, Sir. I just had to be there. That's all."

"Your understanding of all this has been a redeeming feature-and I must say a help to us all. Now, concerning the second, there were two parts to this. As to the first, Nichols was telling me that you were of some help to him and again, not a terrible breach of discipline. But disobedience cannot be condoned and of course you had to be there. Your action in concealing from him what had just transpired, while you were perfectly aware of what to expect, I find commendable too.

Now, as to the last part- this was a most lamentable outburst, Lines, although you stopped yourself before completing it. And if Nichols had not dealt with it as he did, I must say I would be doing so myself, now. However, that is over, and your personal tally of fourteen strokes in the space of less than two hours is something of a record.

Now, we come to the remarkable sequel. I don't need to go into all this Lines-Nichols has done my Pastoral work for me. But just what or who was it leading you into the Chapel today?"

"It's not the first time, Sir. On the day the Headmaster first imposed that Edict, Mark and I were talking for a long time. Then I went along there quietly by myself. You and the Headmaster were at the Alter, still there when I left."

"And you were 'by yourself' you say?" He was shaking his head. "You need not answer that now. One day you will."

Then be brightened up, addressing us both.

"So the Edict is lifted as of now, and you've no need to walk in fear, Lines. Mark will be relieved as well."

Mark was nodding heartily and smiling.

"Thank you, Sir!" We both said.

"So we'll leave it there. There's not often time or opportunity to speak to individuals like this. But you are both doing well. I don't think either of you will see active service against the enemy. The Germans are suffering terribly now, and things will close in faster all the time...

You don't have to take the cloth to serve God, you know. In peacetime England is going to need men like you, Nichols, Passmore, Stirzaker and the rest, able to show moral leadership – against the odds sometimes. Before God! – It's your duty." (He was looking serious again.)

"God bless you both, and have a happy Easter. Your Lent has been hard."
He shook hands with us both and smiled again.

Mark and I were happy as we walked quickly up to the school again; each doing his best to show no emotion although I certainly was almost overwhelmed with relief. There were only about ten minutes left before Hall. There was no Master present so Mark took the meal. I tried to think about the Major but found that I really knew so little. Did he have a family, a personal life, hobbies? I asked a few people, including Dennis. Nobody knew.

Trench Parson, Man of God, Soldier of Jesus Christ, good teacher of Divinity, English, Classics, Pastor to hundreds of young men like us, so many now dead in their prime. They had done their duty.

8 END OF TERM

The last day, Thursday in Holy Week, I awoke after the best night I had had for weeks. The sense of relief was so complete that the pain from the previous day's activity didn't seem to matter and I could be excited about going home without any remaining fear to intrude on my peace. I was up at seven o'clock and eager to check out my bike for the ride home. I had packed almost everything in the cabin trunk for dispatch by rail and then cart to our house in Findon village, and carried only the necessities – my calculus text, tools and an oilskin cycling cape in a small saddle bag with enough space to include my suit, shoes, shirt and tie, planning to wear shorts and T-shirt only on the ride.

The bike was a prized possession, Raleigh, single-speed with high gear ratio, drop handlebars and cable brakes. The bicycle racks were in an old part of the school, across a poorly lit corridor from the "Colds" (as we called the swimming pool). I went along to check brakes, oil the hubs chain and steering, and put air in the tyres with a hand pump. I found several others doing the same thing, all of us excited about the prospect of starting off soon after breakfast, although I knew I had a final appointment with Nurse MacIntosh at eight o'clock.

I was just leaving, pump in hand, when I heard some boys in the Colds area – strictly out of bounds. Therefore, I went to investigate quickly, and found two of the West House juniors. They were immediately silent, and made no reply when I first challenged them. So I looked carefully into the pool and saw a bike in the deep end.

"Whose bike is that?"

"Don't know." – One answered.

"Of course you do. Whose is it? You will answer this if it has to be sticked out of you. – Understand?"

"Seddon's"

"And you two put it there. When?"

"Last night."

"How did you get in? I didn't know it was open."

No answer to that question. So, I asked:

"Are you both biking home?"

"Yes."

"Show me your bikes."

They did so, and I quickly moved mine from its rack, so that my front wheel was between their two back ones, and I used my own chain and padlock to fasten all three bikes together. They would not be going anywhere for quite some time.

"Now," I said, "Breakfast in ten minutes. You will tell Seddon about this, and be back here with towels, cleaning rags, oil, and tools. I have to go to Sick Bay at eight o'clock. When I get back, I want to see you both here, to get that bike out. You will get very cold doing it. So when it is out you can run around the North Field as soon as you are dry, and get warmed up again. Then I will meet you here and you will make that bike perfect. When you have done everything I tell you, you will report to your Housemaster. Understand?"

They were quaking, but I knew very well that I was acting far beyond my authority. I was only an East House prefect and these were West House boys.

"So, you haven't told me yet how you got in here. I thought it was locked."

"Well it was – But we got in."

"Did you break the lock or what?"
"No, we just unscrewed it."

This had not been difficult for them, with right-angled screwdrivers, which they showed me.

"So, we can't lock the place when we leave. Now, after breakfast, find Seddon and you can all wait for me here. Have everything with you to start work. Remember, first of all you will both be stripped off, and diving for it – but not 'til I get back here. I have to go to Sick Bay first. So it will probably be eight fifteen or later. And don't start thinking about my chain. It's hard steel, and a hacksaw will not touch it. Just wait for me at the door. Don't go through it – it is out of bounds."

We all had to hurry to reach our dormitories and dress properly for seven thirty breakfast. The meal was not well attended, as so many had already left. In particular, West House had no prefects remaining. This helped to explain why the boys had felt some confidence in going unpunished. Of the school prefects, Mark, Stirzaker and Beaumont had also left. I was relieved to see Dennis C. Nichols in place at the head of Two North table.

During breakfast, I became even angrier at the enormity of this offence. Seddon, the bike owner, was a small and inoffensive junior boy, who was known to be often the brunt of teasing attacks by others. One of the reasons was that no one could make him fight back. No doubt if he had tried he would have been easily overwhelmed. I felt sympathy with him because of my similar experiences as a new boy and during the whole of my first year. Each of the boys I caught in their bullying act was older, bigger, and much stronger than Seddon. And I imagined what would have been the depth of his chagrin had he not discovered his misfortune until later in the morning, with the bullies departed, and probably no helping hand to retrieve his bike from that eight foot deep, very cold water.

Breakfast over, I tapped Nichols on the shoulder on the way out of Hall, saying:

"I need your help."

He cut me off quickly, saying: "I'm in a rush; I'll see you in Sick Bay in a few minutes."

I had forgotten that I had told him I had this appointment.

Five minutes later, I was already lying prone, as usual, under Nurse MacIntosh's care. She had rebuked me sharply on seeing my rear end.

"Lines! What have you done this time? This looks like two separate assaults – Was it?"

I laughed.

"That's just it. I didn't have to do anything. I had to be there because they were. Didn't we tell you about that?"

She had some idea, but had not had occasion to question

me about it. She became more and more indignant as I unfolded the tale of the Headmaster's Edict – imposed just a few hours after she had first taken me under her care some two and a half weeks ago. Then I told her about the shoe polish episode, and was just laughing with her about this when Dennis came in. I heard him approach the door, and asked her if he might come into the room. On this day, there was no hurry, as no one else had reported sick. Nurse MacIntosh covered the whole area with a towel, and called:

"Yes, Nichols, you can come in." Then she pulled back the towel to expose me completely.

"Alright Lines," she said, "but this must have been two beatings. So there was another one. Tell me about that."

"Well Mr. Collinson did the top one."

"Yes, but the other one is much worse. Who did that?"

"Actually my friend Dennis here, you can't blame him – blame his teacher. He was very well coached."

"What do you mean? Nichols, you can't have studied all this or something. You're such a gentle person."

I had to enlighten her, as she proceeded with pulling off the old dressing to reveal the remaining unhealed small patch. Most of it was bright pink new skin. Dennis said:

"This is the first time I've seen this. Alfred, it's dreadful. It's there for life. Now I can see why you nearly fainted again yesterday. That must have been horribly painful. – I mean my group in the middle."

Poor Dennis! He was red in the face. So, I tried to reassure him.

"Well of course it was. Still is actually. But you know that. And remember how you did Jenkins? He had a hard time with four."

"Nurse, the point is he had caught these boys in rank disobedience – no excuse, and obviously had to stick them all. He was saying – 'Four all round' – which was all it needed, especially as they only had light cotton gym shorts on. But he had never done it before – I told you – you're right – he is a gentle person – and I had this Edict – well he knew he had to include me. So, he asked me a bit about how it was done. I've never done it either. But we used to be able to see our Headmaster at prep school through his study window, and I gave Dennis all the tips I knew on how to make it hurt, although I knew that I would get all the benefit of his practice on the first five, and despite the fact that I was sore already. But I didn't tell him that."

"Why must you boys be so horrid to each other? Lines I hate to say you deserve it – but really! And you're obviously good friends. You're next to each other in Choir."

I said: "We both know that only too well. That's what made it so difficult for Dennis. You've only heard half of the story. This is where it gets complicated. First of all, he brightly suggested that if I had four like the rest he would get accused of being too gentle with them just for my sake. So now, I'm bumped up to five or six. Then out came a copy of the Standing Orders that Dennis follows so closely, and after tantalizing me a little with the details, he told me the writer was MacIntosh. I had no idea he had been killed – didn't occur to me, and I started to say something bad, bad, bad. He was immediately furious, - quite rightly. Then he showed himself up so well. Instead of acting at once, while he was still angry – there was the stick on the table in front of us all – oh yes, he had asked all five of the boys to come back and watch me just as I'd watched them – he turned away from me and talked kindly and respectfully to them about your Cousin – I had not made that connection either. So he allowed himself to cool off completely, before he turned back to me, and said, 'So it's eight, Lines'. Now you can't fault him anywhere. In fact last night the Major was saying to me that if Dennis had not acted like that he would be doing the same himself. Was he (I was referring to her Cousin, now dead) close to you at all? I hardly remember him, although he was Senior Prefect when Dennis and I were new boys. He had been Dennis' House Captain."

Nurse MacIntosh had stopped work, and was sitting there, listening.

"I really didn't know him, 'til I came here before you did – that was just as the war was breaking out. Then when he was lost, about the end of forty-one, we didn't know for a long time whether he was killed or taken prisoner. We slowly became resigned to it.

But I still think you boys are just awful to each other." She sighed and shook her head. I tried to get her to understand.

"Can you just picture that scene in Two North bathroom? It must have a funny side somewhere. But, it was so serious at that time, to us anyway – five boys – all with sore rear-ends standing there to watch me getting it. Dennis and I, each with a face a mile long, clasping hands for mutual reassurance – and me saying: 'Don't shake like that Nichols', and he saying, 'You're shaking too, and so you should be', before he picks up the stick with one fixed idea – Use it! – As hard as possible – to restore respect for your Cousin, Nurse Laurie. That part was not gentle. Be he was right. You should thank him for doing it. He's still a gentle person inside. He felt horrible afterwards. And really we're not horrid to each other very much. I mean some you just couldn't be horrid to – like my friend Little A.J. – Then in contrast there are others you could quite easily, - like D.C. Nichols, for example …" I was laughing now….

"Oh! You boys and your friendship!" she said, and looked away saying slowly, "No wonder this country does so well in a war."

Her eyes were filling, and red. She must have felt more deeply for her Cousin than she allowed.

"So please don't blame Dennis for anything. Actually, we've discussed all this. Last night we were in Chapel together. What a day! And then – I haven't had time to tell Dennis yet, but…"

"I know!" said Dennis "He's lifted that Edict. He told me he was doing that when I went to report those beatings. You know how that's all in the Standing Orders, too. He called you and Mark didn't he? I had been telling him some of the things you had said to me and to those boys, and his eyes were getting bigger all the time. He was saying things like: 'I had no idea' and 'Just remarkable!' He was beaming at me by the time I left."

I told Dennis then how he had said to me: "Nichols has been doing my Pastoral work for me."

Nurse MacIntosh started tidying up and said:

"So you can do it yourself now. It would be much kinder to yourself if you could soak it off in a tub, unless your Mother does it for you."

"No!" I said. "She will never know anything about it. Women don't understand somehow. I mean, suppose you had a son come home from school with this. You would feel awful about it and start to blame yourself. And honestly, what good would that do? It wouldn't change anything. No! I'd hate to see her upset. She's start to cry or something. I couldn't stand that."

Then, as soon as she had finished, Dennis was asking me:

"What's wrong Alfred? Anything I can do?" He was so obviously concerned, and I told him quickly about the boys and Seddon from West House, and how I had acted far beyond my responsibility. He understood at once.

"Let's go there straight away – glad you told me. And don't worry about your authority, Alfred. You're much more known and respected that you realize."

He was just as disturbed as I was by this offence that I had managed to interrupt, and took over the whole situation. We both knew that it was too soon after a heavy meal to go for a cold swim. So we talked to Seddon about what kind of bike it was, and had begun to wonder how much of it would need replacing after a night of immersion in water.

By nine o'clock, we judged it safe. They were in gym clothes for their warm up and recovery run and had towels with them, as well as some clean rags. Dennis gave the order to "Strip off and get it. Be quick now. There's no way round this. Just imagine Seddon doing it by himself with no help."

They went in together and both dived for it. They were shivering and blue as they brought it to the shallow end. Then they propped it up against the wall and jumped out, intending to reach for it. As they got out, Dennis and I watched, while it slipped, rolled and pivoted on one pedal, sliding toward the deep water again.

"Go on back, both of you!" shouted Dennis. We were not going to help at all. They both dived again, and this time one of them held it while the other jumped out and lay on the pool-side to hold it as his friend climbed out to help. By the time they had the bike safely landed they were moving slowly with chattering teeth and slurred speech. These were clear signs, as I would learn years later, of serious hypothermia. Dennis, Seddon, and I had no sympathy. As soon as they were drier, and back into gym clothes, Dennis was putting them through vigorous exercise routines in the changing room. Then they were sent out running round the North Field under my supervision while he went to seek Jacobs, the West Housemaster.

"Jake", as he was known, was in charge of school rugger, having been on the England three-quarter line in the early thirties. He was the school's only Spanish teacher, and these two talents made him a quite indispensable asset. He was not far to seek, as his study was immediately over the Colds, and Dennis guessed correctly that he would be occupied with end-of-term reports. He came down at once and onto the North Field.

He shouted a greeting:

"Lines, thank you for looking after some of my boys again." He was thinking of Little A.J.

However, he was very angry about their behavior. The boys came to him as soon as he appeared, and he was taking the most serious possible view. He said to Dennis and me as they approached:

"How can I reassure parents that there is no bullying in this school as long as this sort of thing happens?" By the time we reached the Colds, Seddon had the wheels off, and was showing us the wreck of the chain with grit all over it, and flecks of fresh rust. The sprockets were red in patches. Then we glanced at the tires, both flat, valves missing.

"Where are the valves?" I asked.

Both boys were looking guilty.
"Still in there."

Jake could hardly control his rage. He had an interest in the grounds, the trees, the golf course, and had taken some responsibility for the pool.

"If either of those gets though the pump foot valve it will ruin the impeller. So! Go in again and get them, now. Is there anything else down there?"

"Spanners and a repair kit."

"Bring them all out."

Then he took Dennis and me aside and we sat on benches while the boys stripped off again. Dennis was quick to reassure him that my Edict was lifted, and Jake was relieved, and shook hands with me.

"Well done Lines! That must been a rough two weeks or more. We've never had that done before, you know. And I'm so glad there was only one beating. From all the previous term-ends I can remember there could have been anything up to six at least." Dennis began to chuckle a little.

"Actually," I said, "there was another one, that Dennis had to look after, and I have to admit – I aggravated that. But yes! – It is a relief. That was one of my first thoughts when I discovered this."

"And from my understanding of you now Lines, you

would not have acted any differently."

"Well, of course not, Sir! This is much too important. It's dreadful" He was nodding.

"Well done both of you!"

"And Lines, you should certainly not be involved any further. Dennis has taken over where you left off, and I'm in the middle. I say middle, because this has to involve their Fathers, and the Headmaster – that is the Major for the time being. I see no reason why they should be here next term, and this means that as far as any good schools are concerned – they're out for life." In the event he sticked them both before they left.

Then he addressed Seddon.

"There's a film of oil over the pool now, and that means all of the bearings are full of water and beyond repair. You need a new bike, and these boys will pay for it – today; needn't be anything fancy, because your old one wasn't. Take a walk down to the village bike shop, and come back to me with a price. I gave them both their pocket money balances yesterday, and I don't remember what there was. They won't have enough to pay for it. But if they have to sell their own bikes and walk home, I'll see to that too."

I said:

"Seddon, you can't go wrong with a Raleigh like mine. I'll show you; simple, quite light, cable brakes, single speed. Come and try it out. Balance is perfect with no hands."

Jake came to look at it as I undid the chain and padlock; he saw the two boys' bikes as well, and took the precaution of removing both valves from each. Little Seddon had to put my seat down, and took the bike round the school and back up the main driveway. He was panting, but delighted. It was good to see him with a smile on his face at last. I said:

"Look, why don't you ride it into the village. It'll save you a lot of time, and I have to do all sorts of things here anyway." We agreed to meet about an hour later.

"You might just find out what the boys could sell theirs for. I'd be delighted to see them walk. I know Evans lives in Horsham. Where does his friend live?"
"Partridge Green – it's about fifteen miles."

"Goody-goody! Evans's Dad was in rugger, too, wasn't he? So, he must know Mr. Jacobs. We won't know what happens until next term."

Seddon got on to my bike again, and turned to say:

"Do you know not many people will know about yesterday's happenings, and they won't till next term either?"

"Never mind, why should they worry? I've thought of all that. We won't be in the Colds 'til about the middle of May. And by that time, all of yesterday's bruises will be gone. Only the scars from Mark left but not to worry; and when the other people see that mess – we can just remind them.

"So you won't forget it, will you?" I said this loudly in Stirzaker's tones.

Seddon, Jake, and Dennis were all laughing.

"Lines!" Said Jake, "We all thank God for your sense of humour." I couldn't help wishing they had all been able to laugh like that three weeks before. But – water under the bridge!

Then Seddon whizzed off towards the village and Dennis and I left poor Jake to handle the wholly ugly mess. In fact neither of us had much to do and walked up to the Tuck Shop for tea. We talked about nothing in particular, both feeling the need for some diversions from school life. We walked slowly back to the Colds. This time Jake was drilling them. After about half an hour, Seddon came back with his report of a bike quite like mine, but not a Raleigh. Jake showed the boys the price and they said they had that much cash in hand. It was more than the balance of the pocket money had been. Therefore, they had been carrying more money on them than any of us usually did. Jake sent them to fetch it, and they returned in a few minutes with every penny needed.

Seddon accepted it, and quickly took his leave. Dennis and I were quick to leave also, and I went to change out for the ride home. We would be going in opposite directions.

9 EASTER '44

The ride home, about twenty seven miles, took me through the village of Cranleigh, and downhill along a "B" road to the Guildford-Horsham A281; then due South along the A24 to Findon village. This had many hills, which were easy to negotiate, except for the long climb up the Bostal, which rises from the rolling Weald to the higher levels of the chalk South Downs. Excitement and an empty stomach kept me going and I enjoyed the early spring, in and out of a soft drizzle. The last two miles before the village was concrete road, with two lanes each side of the bushy median. The surfaces had been spoiled by the passage of tanks, which had left a maze of cracks in them.

The village itself is ancient. The old coach route used to pass a half mile further to the West, and over the past thousand years the centre of the village has moved to the present site, leaving the Parish Church and Cemetery, formerly central features, separated from other buildings by what was now ploughed land and lanes. The village migration has continued, leaving the main A24 route to pass by it on the West side.

I turned East, off the A24 through the village and out to the hamlet of Nepcote, on a slope approaching Cissbury Ring, where our house, Carna, was the last on a chalk-road leading on to the Downs – a beautiful, peaceful location.

Cissbury Ring has a long history, little known with accuracy. The top has several pre-Roman mounds, probably old flint-mines. The "Ring" is roughly elliptical and has the classic Roman fossa and vallum, with two entry points. There are two old baggage roads spiraling up to these entrances, and the view from the top is strategically commanding. On a clear day, the Seven Sisters and Beachy Head can be seen to the East, and the Isle of Wight to the West. By this stage of the war access to the hill was prevented by a deep tank trap excavated in the chalk about a hundred feet below the fossa, and by a belt of barbed wire with a few notices: "Danger-mines" posted. There was a single sentry armed with a rifle at each of only two gaps in this fortification. Several weapons pits had been dug and sandbagged and we could see (with binoculars) that a length of iron drainpipe was projecting from each of these – it may have looked like a gun-barrel to a highflying German reconnaissance camera. Moreover, we learned later that the "mines" did not exist. When the whole scene was being put together the rumour put out was that the guns up there were French "seventy-five's", well – proved field guns from the First Great War.

I reached home just as Mother, Father, and Mother's Mother (Madge) were finishing lunch, and I learned that my sister, Mary (known at home as "Joy") was expected the next day. She had read History at Royal Holloway College, and was at work at Bletchley Park; she was living nearby at Leighton Buzzard, and entertaining American air force officers at a Red Cross Club in Bedford in her spare time. She remained mute about the nature of her work, under the Official Secrets Act, until her death in '99.

Routines at home were simple. Mother would rest after lunch until tea – time about four o'clock. Father was usually occupied with lock designs, Grandma would read and do crochet work and I was free to study.

After tea, there was the dog to exercise, and some work bringing home and cutting firewood. In the evening, we lit the kerosene lamps, which were our only means of lighting, and Mother would cook a simple meal, using the twin oil-burner stove. We went to bed with a candle or hurricane buttie.

I had written home to tell my parents of the promotion to house prefect rank, and to tell them that the Headmaster was interested in my up-coming exam. I had told them also that I was trying to join the Fleet Air Arm; although, if the latter plan succeeded, the whole Naval Architecture career would have to wait until after the war. Soon after reaching home, I told them about the events of that morning, and mentioned the shoe polish incident of the previous day, omitting my part in it. Likewise, I told them nothing of the run and the matters of Nichols and MacIntosh.

Meanwhile, Mother had had a hysterectomy, and in her post-operative period had had a "collapse" episode with chest pain, and a grossly swollen leg. These must have been the deep vein thrombosis and pulmonary embolism that imposed such morbidity and mortality on surgery survivors at that time. Neither my sister nor I realized then how close we had been to losing her.

Joy seldom talked about her American friends, but she had lost many. The American air force was suffering a severe beating from German fighters. In addition, whereas a big British bomber had a crew of five, and each navigated independently at night, an American B17 had up to eleven men on board, and they would fly by day in large formations, with lead aircraft navigating, so that their air crew losses were the more serious.

I was able to start studying immediately. The exam was to be about ten days after Easter, in Cambridge. Most of my school holidays had had some kind of exam cloud over them since the age of eleven. So, I was quite used to sitting at a table in my bedroom – the only room on the top floor, for much of each day, except for time out to gather wood, ride a bike down to the village shops, or walk the dog.

On Good Friday, Joy arrived looking exhausted, and spent much of that weekend sleeping. I made some inquiries about Church services for that day and for Easter. At this time, I used often to bike into Worthing for the morning and sometimes an evening service at the Congregational Church. My Mother had been married there in 1920, and our next-door neighbours at Carna were two Aldridge spinster sisters. Their brother was a bass in the Congregational Church, and we used to wonder how we might be related. Madge Camburn had married Alfred Aldridge about 1884, and had two children, Dulce, who died of meningitis in infancy, and my Mother, Gwendolen in '97, twelve years later. These daughters and their father Alfred had what we call in our family the "Aldridge thumb". Both thumbs have hyper-extension to a right angle at the inter-phalangeal joint. I have this also, and so did our neighbours, the Aldridge sisters, and my middle-aged bass friend, another Alfred. It was interesting. Yet, none of us had the time or inclination to pursue lineage.

Nevertheless, on this Sunday I went to Easter Matins at the village Church. I always look forward to the welcoming, familiar cadences of Cranmer.

"Dearly beloved, the Scripture moveth us in sundry places…"

The little choir at this Church was a delight. There were four or five women, all good readers, and we had no difficulty with Anglican Chant and Coverdale's Psalter. We did two canticles at Matins. I was the only male, and two of the women were strong contraltos. I well remember finding that in the Psalm one Sunday my reciting note was strongly dissonant with the soprano, by one tone. So I took the easy course and joined the top line for the reciting note. After the service one of the altos came to me to complain:

"What a pity you funked that beautiful third inversion of the Dominant seventh. It would have been lovely. Ah well! Next time perhaps!"

I used to be much more shy about my voice in those years. I had not started to play with it as I did later.

The Church was well attended. We had some of the well-known Easter hymns. It was not easy to accept clearance from the shame I still felt about MacIntosh. However, I was able to give thanks for the support I had been given so freely and, I had to acknowledge, lovingly by those men of God, Loveday, Crowhurst, and little Dennis C. Nichols.

Mother was slow in convalescence, and beset by continued swelling of the whole left lower limb. There were no firm elastic stockings at that time, or even elastic bandages. She would bind it up firmly with cotton bandages and wear a close-fitting lisle stocking over this. At every opportunity, she would put the leg up on something. Also, there was no use of any anti-coagulant then. Even the benefit of Aspirin in this condition was not yet applied. But she followed advice carefully, taking frequent short walks and using stairs often. Our stair-case at Carna was ideal for her, because of its gentle gradient, having a rise of about five inches for a run of ten at each step.

Joy and I, often with Father also, now aged sixty-eight, used to go for walks of a few miles at a time over the green hills and soft Sussex turf. I would carry a woomera, and use it to throw an iron-tipped bamboo spear over the three-phase grid transmission lines, which carried one hundred and thirty-three kilovolts, confident that I would never manage to hit one of them. The iron tip had been forged, while we watched, at the village smithy, with a coke fire and manual bellows.

This was in the fifth year of war, and England was one huge armed camp. We had increasing numbers of Canadians and Americans. Both of these nations had well designed, if not tailored, uniforms for officers and other ranks contrasting with the coarse, hard-wearing battle-dress of the British. And whereas the British private had three shillings per day, the Canadians were paid the equivalent of eight shillings and sixpence and the Americans thirteen shillings. This led to animosity in the pubs and such eating places as there were. Canadians and Americans were given food of much higher quality than could be obtained in any English restaurant.

Social contacts with these boys were continually difficult for English girls. A respectable girl could befriend a young man to whom she had been appropriately introduced. It was best if the parents knew each other before the young people met. For a man to speak to a girl in a pub, for example, was certainly deprecated. Only a low-class girl, or bar-maid or prostitute would allow such a "pickup" to happen. Consequently, seldom did a Canadian or American male befriend any cultured or well-bred English girl.

My sister, however, had her own ideas and standards. She had been known for wearing the shortest skirts in Royal Holloway College, and at five-foot-ten inches height, was able to carry this manner of dress well. In fact, the following year she visited me in St. John's College Cambridge, whose boat club, the Lady Margaret, had been responsible for the introduction of the word "Blazer" to the language for its bright scarlet jacket. She used my Lady Margaret scarf to make a skirt, with the scarf width as the total skirt length. Joy made a series of friends in her hostess work, but was wise enough to avoid a close attachment to any. For their life expectation was short. Also she was perpetually conscious of her responsibility to maintain total secrecy, and would not allow any possibility of compromise in this.

At school we had often discussed the American fighting men, and despised them for many reasons. Most of them were, by our standards, fat. We could not imagine them coping with our obstacle courses or putting up with the privations of trenches and foxhole life. We ridiculed the way they seemed to surround themselves with luxury, sumptuous food, mechanized kitchens and laundry services, and so much road transport. When we saw them at drill, we would laugh aloud. They were hopelessly sloppy about it. In addition, their respect for officers seemed abysmal. However they began to prove themselves in action against the enemy. Later we all admired the way Canadians slogged through Northern France and the Low Countries and carried the terrible fighting in the Schelt estuary and Walcheren.

Civilian life was bleak, and had been so for four years. Food rationing, introduced on the eighth January 1940, had been severe at times with:
Butter – 2 oz
Cheese – 2 oz – with extra for manual and farm workers
Margarine – 2 to 4 oz
Meat varying sometimes down to 4 oz.

These were the weekly amounts. Potatoes could be had. Bread was not rationed at all or scarce during the whole war. It took a Socialist Government, after the war, to produce a scarcity of bread also, and ration it – for the only time in English history.

All consumer goods were scarce. Such as were made were of poor quality, with the slogan "War finish" permitting and encouraging this. No cars were produced after 1939. The blackout was all-pervading. Vehicles travelling at night were allowed a slit aperture in each headlight about four inches long and a quarter inch in height. There was no street lighting. Road names were all removed. So were all the signposts. The name at each railway-station was nowhere to be seen. A platform worker would call out the station name through a hand-held megaphone as each train pulled in.

Instead of bright advertisements, there were notices –

"Careless talk costs lives."

"Never pass on a rumor."

"Is your journey really necessary?"

"Take your holidays at home."

"Dig for victory. Grow your own food."

"Make do and mend."

...And more like these.

I had been looking forward to the trip to Cambridge. This involved a journey from Worthing to Victoria on the Southern Railway, an all-electric route with third rail power pick up that had been installed in the immediate post-depression boom of the early thirties, and engineered so well that it has survived almost unchanged. There was a tube-train to cross London to Liverpool Street. This had been electrified before the first war and had stood the tests of time and hard use for still longer. Finally, there was a London and North Eastern Railway steam train out to Cambridge. This was quite different - slow to accelerate, dirty, noisy. Nevertheless, it had been the accepted norm for travel for three or more generations.

I reached Cambridge in the evening and the exams were the following day. At the simple B & B establishment there was a knock on the door in the morning, and a maid called out:

"Water sir!"

There was an enamel jug of hot water placed on the floor outside the door, for ablution at the wash-hand basin in the bedroom.

The exam involved a three-hour paper in the morning and, after a short lunch break, another three-hour paper in the afternoon. Immediately after it was over we started discussing the questions, and I was surprised to find how poorly many of my fellow-candidates had fared. The exam was not competitive, but was known to have a poor pass rate, usually well below fifty per cent.

When it was over, I briefly considered the beautiful surroundings and old chapels and colleges. But these things did not remove a longing to be home again.

Even in wartime, Cambridge was beautiful. Yet it had not occurred to anyone that it might be possible to clean old stonework, and all were content with the blackness from hundreds of years of domestic coal-smoke and charcoal-fire cooking. Markets had been lit by the smoky flame from tow-poles. These were long poles, each with a bundle of rags and rope tied at one end, soaked in tow and tar, and served to prolong business hours past twilight. When their sputtering died the market closed. In addition, most of the valuable stained glass, including the whole of King's East window, had been removed, and stored against the possibility of bomb damage.

So, I caught a train south as soon as I could, only to find that I had reached Victoria after the last train had left. I slept fitfully on a bench with my head on a small back-pack: and took the early newspaper train South. Refreshment during the night was tea at two pence, or coffee at three pence. There was powdered milk in the tea. However, there was no sugar. Everyone had to carry a bottle of saccharin tablets.

I remember little about that holiday, except that Joy had to return to Bletchley all too soon, and that my results came quickly. I had passed. At once I was longing to tell Peter

Stirzaker about this, and was able to enjoy a few days of freedom before returning to school for my last term.

10 SUMMER TERM '44

This was the most enjoyable time of my school life. At last, I had no exam pressure. I was half-heartedly hoping for a distinction in Physics, but did not need it, and there were other things to enjoy.

Soon after arriving at the school I attended the Headmaster's study to report having passed the Mechanical Sciences Qualifying Exam. He was genuinely pleased, and then pointed out that I would also need a small Latin exam for Cambridge University. He was looking through my academic record, and found no Latin credit in the School Certificate.

"A scholar without a Latin Credit! Not worth your salt! Why is that?"

"We had to do eight hundred lines of the Aeneid, Sir. I would have passed the unseen easily enough. But we were all entered in Latin Book." (My face was going red, I believe).

"Ah yes, Mr. Plassis' class - no discipline! If only we had been able to help him like we did Mr. Wicks, so many people might have done better." He turned to me with a trace of a smile. I was relieved.

"So you had better join my five A Latin classes." He was still looking at the record: "I see you had the highest aggregate mark that year. But there was no top scholarship."

"I was awarded the third," I said. He put the record away, and changed the subject.

"I was unwell at the end of Lent. However, the Major kept me well informed, and Mr. Jacobs told me some more. You had an eventful last two days. And I understand that you and Nichols D.C. have struck up a friendship in the course of all this."

"I wish I had known him before, Sir. We had been sitting together in the Chapel for two years and hardly spoken to each other."

"Lines, you must learn to appreciate your faults and be on your guard. You have plenty of intelligence and a ready wit, as well as some other attributes that have shown up well and have been used for the benefit of others. But it was your tongue that brought you grief twice during Lent. There is a passage in James that will help you. Will you read it, and make it a matter of prayer?"

"Thank you Sir. I should. I'm sure."

So Loveday was still quite convinced that I was at that time a "Believer". On looking back to those years, I do not fully understand how I can have been so reluctant to make a firm decision or commitment.

Loveday's Latin classes were interesting. He was often surprised at the extent of my vocabulary, and some exchanges were even amusing. I remember how in one class he labored a point of construction, it seemed ad nauseam, and then had us write some sentences to prove our understanding. So I complied patiently, and then wrote, underneath one required sentence, an alternate construction for the same meaning-recalled from Mr. F.G.Turner's own "Grey Book:" of Latin syntax pearls which he had given to us at Tormore in 1940. I had written:

"Fortior fuit quam ut occissus sit."

The Head came round looking over our shoulders in turn, and marking ticks or crosses as appropriate. On seeing mine, he said:

"Oh, yes, quite right! And you've done it a clever way too as well as the one I was teaching you. Where did you learn that?"

"At prep school Sir."

"Four years ago! You must have a retentive memory."
From that time, I was "teacher's pet" of five A Latin and had to take great care to excel in all his classes. The Cambridge University "Littlego" Latin exam was easy.

There were some important changes in the school. John Mark had left, and Peter Stirzaker was formally appointed Senior Prefect. Beaumont had started his training earlier than expected, and my contemporary I.G. Tait was our new House Captain. Nichols was still with us for Two North, and young J.A. Tait was one of the West House prefects.

I moved into number one study with Tait, and Sutton. Fairsbarns, Trace and Flynn were in number two. My other contemporary, Ransom had still no promotion, and was occupied with trying to add enough credits in the School Certificate to matriculate and move into the sixth form. He was a quite charming person, never worried by his repeated academic failures. Nigel Ransom and Ian Tait had been firm friends since their arrival together and placement in Middle C. Ransom could never cut the nails on his right hand, and for the whole four years that we were together, he would approach Ian Tait with a pair of scissors in the houseroom or elsewhere so that Ian could cut all his right hand nails for him. This continued even when Ian had reached school prefect status while Nigel still had no rank.

Sports in the summer were cricket, with games or net practice on most days, and track and field sports. Of the latter, javelin and discus had not happened since before the war. There was no teaching in high jump. The shot put remained, with a twelve-pound shot for seniors and an eight –pound for juniors and intermediates. These were genuine naval cannon balls, well over a hundred years old. The practice track was a quarter-mile on grass, and beside it was a six-lane straight for the one hundred yards. For each age group, there were a lower and a higher standard at each distance. Achieving a lower standard earned a point for one's house. A higher standard earned two points and a place in heats. Since one had only two tries at each distance it was best to train and practice well before going against the stop-watch. For training we preferred to go out on the Long Junior route. Sutton, Ransom, and I would go together. Tait ran alone. Peter Stirzaker had various companions, but would easily out- run most of them. Fairbarns would sometimes start with him, and have to fall back after a mile or so.

Peter became wonderfully fit. He was able to equal the school record at two hundred and twenty yards (a furlong) and looked beautiful doing it - far ahead of the field every time. This was so much the more creditable due to the fact that he was seventeen, whereas most of our records had been set by boys of eighteen, and a few of nineteen, the peacetime leaving ages. He could have picked any distance for heats, but no one was allowed more than two. He was content with the one hundred and the two-twenty, and won both finals easily. He based his sprinting on Jesse Owens who had won the Munich Olympic four hundred in '36. His whole upper body and limbs were relaxed, as if any energy diverted from lower limbs could detract from the main purpose - to put the yards of ground behind him. This led to the appearance of floating easily at speed, so far removed from the aggressive, hyped up, tension-state sprinting we see today.

By contrast, I had to train hard to reach the higher standards at five-thirty for a mile and sixty seconds for the quarter. (The current school record at the four-forty was forty-seven point nine seconds).

We had plenty of space on the school playing fields. There was enough area to mark out ten separate rugger fields. Heats and finals were run on the large Jubilee Field, with the quarter mile track at the Western, or Pavilion end. The one mile started with four runners in line abreast, with a two-hundred yard converging approach to the midpoint of the North side of the ellipse. The one hundred and the two-twenty had six lanes abreast dead straight, South of the main ellipse, without encroaching upon it.

By about the middle of May we began to feel the heat, and questions were asked about swimming. Could we start using the Colds? Already Tait and Trace and I had been running out to a disused quarry, and started swimming there, going in with running shorts only, and drying off on the run home. It was too cold for most, but exhilarating and not many boys even knew the place existed. Had it become common knowledge it would certainly have been ruled "out of bounds". But Jake had done his work well, and allowed us three to try out the Colds. The water was clear and at least as cold as our quarry. We each did a few lengths fast while he watched, and judged it nearly warm enough to open for the houses to use once weekly. Another ten days allowed it to warm up a little more, and during this time, we three were the only people using it. We were about equally fast, at seven seconds per length, and usually did no more than ten. A rota was arranged with each house having one swim night per week. On that night after dormitory prayers the order: "Colds" was given, and the house prefect for the week supervised the swim. It fell to me to take them in on our first house night – our day was a Wednesday.

The whole house was there, including Ian Tait and Trace. I realized that I was now showing off my bright pink stripes, as well as one last, densely adherent scab. There was not a murmur or hint of disrespect. I arranged them three breast, and said:

"Right, Tait and Trace and I will do two lengths. Then everyone does two. After that it will be a free swim 'til twenty past nine."

So we three led the way and made sure everyone else followed. Only one or two went back for a few more lengths with us. Then, just before twenty past nine I gave the order:

"All out … dry quickly. Don't be late at the bell."

Then Ian Tait said loudly: -

"Now listen! Everyone has been polite. If you want to swim fast, copy Lines' crawl. What else do you notice when he's doing it?"

At last, they felt free to laugh, as Tait and I were doing.

"That's right! His ass is a mess isn't it? Now does everyone remember what all that was about? Tell me."

"Disrespect for…" several people answered.

"Yes!" said Tait. "And you won't forget it will you."

Cries of, "NO!"

So, we had cleared the air, and the lesson of last term was well remembered. Even Peter would have laughed if he had been there. By this time, he was well aware that his words had passed almost into the school fabric. He was known to be strict, but was liked as well as respected.

"Brace up!" I said. "Seven minutes to the bell."

I had to be the last out and lock the place up. It was tidy and clean.

As the bell went at half past nine, I looked round quickly. No one late in bed; I picked up the clip-board.

"No one on the list tonight – Well done! Stand by windows! Lights out! Tuck under! Open windows! Good night and God Bless!"

It was a happy house. By this time, the new boys in every house had been made aware of the events of the Lent term. The bullies were gone and forgotten, and Miss Simpson and old Mr. Wicks were well appreciated and respected.

Little A.J. came up to me after Matins one day. He hadn't grown much but was looking better than I had ever seen him. He started telling me how some of the other juniors had been giving him a bad time last term but that this attitude seemed to have changed. I was glad that he didn't start talking about the events of the last Wednesday of term. That was all so complicated, and I didn't really feel free to talk about it with anyone except perhaps Dennis and Nurse Laurie. They did not bring it up either. However, the warm three-way friendship remained.

I had duly reported to Nurse Laurie at Sick Bay on the first morning of the new term, and she simply glanced at the remaining scab and re-covered it with zinc oxide and a simple flannel dressing and sticky tape. After this, she wanted to see me only twice each week. She was as surprised as I was to find how long it was taking, and one day I asked Dr. Gordon. He simply shrugged his shoulders, saying that we could expect the last slough to fall off at three months. Nurse Laurie was totally forgiving. She asked: "Did you have a good Easter? I was pleased to hear about the exam." She had seen the Headmaster posting my results on his notice-board, with a smile on his face.

I began to give more time to leisure reading, now that the pressure was off. East House Library had some bound copies of "Sea Breezes" magazine dating from the inter-war years, and I sought out articles and stories on old sailing ships. From these and from the diagram of square rig in the 1928 Encyclopedia Britannica I acquired an extensive knowledge and understanding of details of sail making, and of standing as well as running rig. It is an interesting fund of information that I have retained throughout life.

House prefect rank carried with it the need to forgo some of my former activities. For instance, I decided to bow out of the group of fifth and sixth form chemistry students known amongst us as the "Science Society". During the previous two terms we had studied various explosives and fuses, and worked out quantities for some remarkably effective small bombs. Our gun-powder was at first the classic potassium nitrate, flowers of sulphur and charcoal, which we later modified, adding aluminum powder for a better flash detonation, and substituting potassium chlorate for some of the saltpeter. Our favorite fuse was potassium permanganate and glycerine. All these substances were easily obtained over the counter at any small Chemist's shop. It was easy to fill a small empty Brasso pot with one of our explosives, and then at leisure to add some Condie's crystals to a drop of household glycerine, screw these together in a toffee paper and put it in the pot. Then, after screwing the lid on there was time to throw the pot and turn away, looking innocent until there was this loud bang with a flash and a puff of smoke.

"I wonder what that was." – And other stupid comments followed. We had certain rules. One was to keep receipts for all the chemicals we bought, as the possibility of being caught in the act was ever present, and we had to be able to prove that none of our materials had been stolen from the school chemistry lab.

On returning to school in the summer, I had considered my position at first in an ambivalent manner. I had contracted to bring with me some supplies, especially of aluminum powder and potassium chlorate. So, I did as I had said I would, but then simply handed all my supplies to Wray, of Two and Three South, who was eager to take them over, as well as the receipts from "Avon – Chemist – Findon Valley". Wray was also a house prefect, but had no timidity about him, and continued to experiment with his devices on Smithfield Common.

In fact, the Home Guard was hardly more advanced than we were. There was an antitank weapon, more primitive than the Bazooka, which fired a stone ginger-beer bottle. The barrel was a length of a light steel pipe about three inches in diameter. It was muzzle – loaded with a small cordite charge, a wad of cotton and its bottle. Firing was by a simple trigger and percussion cap. The bottle contained petroleum, liquid latex, and white phosphorus. When fired it was aimed at the upwind side or end of a tank, and broke upon impact. The white phosphorus ignited on contact with air. The petroleum provided a hot spectacular blaze and the latex a white, acrid smoke. The hope was that this combination would cause the crew to evacuate their vehicle, coughing, choking and half blinded, to be forthwith dispatched by rifle or shot gun fire, or clubbed, piked or cut down my an means the angry Home Guardsmen could bring to bear. The Home Guard, probably the cheapest army ever raised had many veterans of the First Great War, who had never abandoned their belief that the only good German was a dead one, and had not forgiven the next generation for failing to hold the same opinion. They were unpaid, poorly armed, and were glad to see the lowly ginger- beer bottle raised to the exalted status of Hun-buster.

However, Wray overstepped the safety margin. He had fashioned a large but very simple bomb that he could screw into any light-bulb fitting, and one day went into the main school lavatories, turned the main light switch off and replaced one of the bulbs with his device. He had included plenty of sawdust for live sparks, and a small excess of charcoal for smoke. Then while he and Faithful were strolling about the entrance, with studied innocence on their faces, two people arrived in quick succession, one a junior boy who headed straight into the darkened lavatories, and just after him Monty Aldridge, the senior Science teacher. The boy evidently found the switch, for there was a flash and a bang and he emerged rapidly, pursued by smoke. Monty at once seized Faithful. But as he did so, Wray came forward saying:

"Not his at all Sir! It was mine."

Wray's bomb was inordinately big, and could have been destructive if carefully placed or in a confined space. But he had taken care to place it in the most distant socket, about fifty feet beyond the light switch, in a place where there were tiled concrete walls separating five lavatories on each side of an open space. The whole place was innocent of doors. There was no window or skylight. The bomb had no fragments or shrapnel, but was deliberately contained in a cardboard toilet-roll centre so that no damage would occur. So, the maker had satisfied himself as to its safety, with distance and the muffling effect of the concrete partitions to lessen the blast.

Monty took Wray at this word, which was easy to

believe, as he was still holding in his left hand the light bulb, which he had just removed before replacing it with his device. The ensuing procedure was on the "stick first, talk after" principle, and Wray was then eager to divulge the whole of his calculations. His bomb had contained one gram-molecule of potassium chlorate with enough sulphur to burn to the dioxide plus aluminum powder for flash effect and some charcoal powder for smoke. Since this amounted to nearly half a pound it could have been lethal. Monty was quick to understand this. At the end of the short interview, Wray was still writhing from eight strokes, although Monty was known to be not very good at it. Punishment was thought to have been adequate, and proved to be so, as no further explosive experiments were carried out, and the Society disbanded.

For my part, I was glad that Monty had not demanded to see the receipts, as my name was on them. That was a close call.

Smoking was a continuing problem amongst the older boys, and could compromise any prefect's position and authority. It was forbidden, and always treated with the stick, although not regarded as a serious offence. Among the East House prefects, Stirzaker, with his passion for fitness, was known to be quite stern in his attitude. Tait had smoked a little before his promotion and wisely given it up. Sutton continued to smoke, and had brown-stained fingers. He had never been caught in the act. My own position was simple, as I had simply tasted it once, hated it, and never tried it again. So, in our No. 1 study Tait had made it clear to Sutton that if he were ever caught the stick would follow in short order.

One day Ransom and Sutton started to question my attitude. Sutton asked:

"How much do you really hate smoking, Alfred?"

"I hate the taste of the stuff myself. Only tried it once, and don't want to do it again."

"But what about anyone else; us for instance?"

"It's forbidden. That's all there is to it."

"So if I started smoking you'd report me, you mean?"

"It's obvious that you smoke. Your fingers are stained, and your clothes smell of it."

"So that makes me guilty! What are you going to do about it?"

"Nothing, 'til I catch you at it. And you must realize that is bound to happen, sooner or later."

"And then you'll report me. So you really would do your best to get another house prefect sticked."

"Certainly, and since I've been a friend of yours for years, the very last thing I ought to do is throw you any favours!"

Ramson joined in: -

"Now we're getting down to it. It's duty and all that I suppose. Just like your good friend Stirzaker. England expects, and so on."

"Exactly, just like my good friend Peter Stirzaker. But I have the greatest possible admiration for him, so don't start to belittle him in my ears please. What do you know about him anyway? Are you referring to that famous challenge of his and the 'you won't forget it will you?' Bit?"

"No! Before that. Don't you realize? Everybody knows what his attitude was when you turned up in one North bathroom by yourself."

"I don't know how that got out. He had a bad time over that, for a while anyway. Look! Why don't you both make it easier for us all by just not smoking? If you go on, you are sure to be caught, and action then is automatic. No one will worry about it. They will just get the stick out, because – yes! That is what is expected, and it will therefore take place."

"He seems to mean what he says," said Sutton.

"Too bad!" said Ransom

"You bastard!" They both said, and they evidently meant this.

"Yes, I know. But now that you know, just watch it."

Sutton found difficulty believing this. However, within a few days another of my friends, a house prefect from One and Four South, was caught in the act and appropriately treated. So the non-smoking fraternity made their point, at least for the time being.

About nine boys from the school, including I.G. Tait, Trace and I were invited to the R.N.V.R. offices in Cockspur Street, off Trafalgar Square, for interviews and medicals on the same day. We were all excited about this. Ian and Trace were going for Y-scheme, and I was trying for Fleet Air Arm. So much depended on the reports and recommendations from the Housemaster. Ian Tait was obviously well placed with house colours in Rugger, Hockey and Fives, his House Captain rank and a good record on the School shooting team. He was small of stature and assertive by nature – qualities which are highly valued in the Navy. Trace was also good at games, with house colours. I was despondent in this company, as my performance in games was so poor.

Nevertheless, Blackshaw had written something about 'fearless honesty – absolute integrity- initiative…' And these were words that denoted 'Officer – like qualities'. He certainly knew the jargon required. Perhaps Jake had been talking to him or even the Major, the Rev. N. Crowhurst.

So my interview went well, and I tried to show no surprise as their words were read out, as if that were the very least that I expected. But, I did badly on the medical. The Doctor said nothing about a heart murmur, but found one eye slightly different from the other, and then failed me out right for flying because I was unable to breathe through one nostril.

However, I was glad to be accepted for the Navy, and the three of us from East House went to celebrate at Lyon's Corner House close by. I was still hoping to get into small craft, perhaps M.T.B.s although the most probable destiny would be Corvettes. Personal preference counted for almost nothing. Looking further ahead, any sea experience would help me in the competition for Royal Corps of Naval Constructors.

The V-1, or flying bomb, period gave us a renewed sense of the nearness of the war. We realized that a Channel crossing must come soon, as the build-up of American, Canadian and British troops in the South of England increased. Those of us who had been at the school in September 1940 remembered clearly how the daylight air activity had not ceased when the great air battles over Kent and Sussex stopped happening. We had been told how the R.A.F., far from resting at home to lick its wounds, had taken the battle, with no break in continuity, to the Channel coast and Northern France, daily strafing and bombing invasion barges, harbours and airfields, while the German fighters so often remained grounded, a truly defeated force.

There had followed a series of night raids on London and other cities, against which we had at first almost no defense. We had seen the burning of London from sixty miles for three nights in succession. As the war progressed we heard and saw less of the Luftwaffe. Single German planes were often heard at night - their twin engines were not synchronized, and they gave out an irregular, beating tone.

"One of theirs" we would say, and usually ignored it.

On some clear nights a few of us would be out on the North Field, watching while searchlights poked at the sky, and were always delighted when a plane was caught in a beam. No amount of twisting and diving could provide escape from the searchlights once they had lit up the enemy, and within a few minutes we saw a burst of tracer, usually followed by the sight of a burning aircraft falling. We always cheered.

My mother, at the age of about nineteen, had seen a German Zeppelin shot down in flames at Cuffley and remembered for life the roar of delight that went up from all over London, when it was seen. On each of two previous nights there had been many killed by bombs dropped from these airships. Nearly thirty years had passed and the human reaction was the same.

Now these same Huns, or rather the sons and grandsons of the crew of the "Cuffley Zep" were entertaining us with pop-pop popping flying bombs. Again, the Germans had out-paced our defences and we had to improvise all manner of ways to live with the new threat.

Each day, a house prefect had to have a rota of spotters prepared. There would be two at a time on the roof of the old building, listening, and peering southward. Each boy did two hours, and there was a change of one at each hour. Their orders were to record every V-1 they saw or heard, with a rough estimate of the distance by which the line of flight would miss the school; If the distance were judged less than a quarter of a mile, they would press two bells to sound an alarm. Repeated short jabs were the warning. A continuous note was "All Clear". The spotters would remain on the roof, and if they were looking upward at the ugly little aircraft at an angle steeper than forty-five degrees, as it passed, this judgment had been correct (they were set to fly at an altitude of a thousand feet). They were then to guess the angle and record it.

In general, this was an enjoyable way for most boys not merely to miss a few classes, but to feel part of the war. However my friend Ransom was using the spotters' perch as a smoking haven. I guessed this was happening, but never managed to catch him in the act, although I had found him up there more than once when he was not on the rota. One day, evidently Blackshaw and I had the same idea, and I was running up the East House stairway on my way to check on my spotters, when I overtook him. I said: "Sometimes I find an extra person up there, Sir, and I want to discourage this." I had hardly spoken when Ransom appeared. Blackshaw stopped and addressed him simply:

"I put it to you, Ransom that you were smoking up there."

Without hesitation Ransom said:-"Yes Sir, I was"

"I'll see you in the bathroom here in a few minutes," he said, "I just have to go and get something."

We turned round and walked past West House dormitory to the new building, where he was of course going to his study to fetch a cane.

"That was a bow at a venture. What?" He said. (I Kings

XXII.34)

I had to congratulate him. However, of course, I was delighted with the way Ransom had responded. Here was not a trace of disdain for the idea of "duty" or of falling short of England's expectation. He had risen to the occasion himself, at once. In fact, Blackshaw wasn't very good at beatings as he left several seconds between the strokes, and his wife had told us, at the Literary Society meeting one evening, that he sometimes went home for a tot of Whiskey after doing it. Nevertheless, Ransom seemed to think it adequate and gave up the habit, at least for that summer.

Later I went to congratulate him:

"Well done Nigel! I'm glad it didn't have to be me that caught you."

Then to my surprise, he started to thank me, although I hadn't been very kind or careful in talking to him about it. He finally said: "It's not what you say to people that matters so much, Alfred. It's just that quite a lot of people want to copy you."

Perhaps those scars were worthwhile to a few other people. But I was still wishing the pain would just stop coming back.

Our good friend Sutton, however, was unmoved. Tait and I were bothered by the smell on his clothing, and we both thought he was compromising his house prefect status so long as he continued. Ian broached the subject with Peter Stirzaker, who saw no problem at all. He simply said:

"O.K. Search! Is he there now? Better if he is when we do it."

This was just after supper one day - ideal time. So the

three of us went up to our No. 1 study shortly before prep - starting bell at half past seven. Ian opened his door for Peter, and we followed. Sutton was starting already on some French work. Peter said:-

"Sutton, we all know you smoke. So, show me all your supplies and we'll help you get rid of them."

Sutton acquiesced at once, going bright red in the face as he uncovered some cartons in a desk drawer.

Peter said: "Is that all?"

"Yes."

"Well, you know what happens now. So, I it's not all, better show us the rest, because it would be so tedious to have to go through this tomorrow – all over again after a thorough search. Of course this study is not the only place we'll be searching."

Sutton said nothing.

"So, meet me in the bathroom in ten minutes, and bring all the supplies to me there. I'll be asking a few more questions. So we'll help you clear your head first."

Ian Tait and I were both feeling guilty for having not done this ourselves. Sutton excused himself, saying:

"I'll have to go and get them."

Peter shut the door after him, and turned to us.

"Now, why did you let this go on for so long? You should both know better. Lines – you know all about that Edict of Compassion thing, don't you? Don't you think something like that ought to apply now – to both of you? You've been sharing his guilt for weeks, - covering for him actually, Come on! I want some answers."

We were both surprised by this outburst. Of course, Peter was quite right. We nodded in agreement. That wasn't enough for Peter.

"So, what happens now?"

I said: -

"Everything you've just said is absolutely true. So there is nothing for us to say, really. We just have to ask you what you want to do and fall into line."

"Correct. Meet me up there, with Sutton. You get three each, and he gets six. If you had not asked me first, you might have had the same as he's getting."

Ian and I walked up there slowly, and he was getting angrier all the way.

"Isn't he as much at fault as we are – for not acting sooner?"

"Maybe he was being kind to us like we were with Sutton and Ransom."

"That's another thing, Alfred. Blackshaw didn't want to punish you did he, and another thing too, - what about all the other smokers in the school? He ought to be searching all the house prefects' studies."

"Well, Janes certainly searched Two and Three South studies. He found a stash and caned two of theirs yesterday. You heard?"

"No." said Ian. "I didn't know that. We'd better put him on to Flynn."

"You bet," I said, "or we'll be guilty again. There's some truth in what you're saying – but not enough to let us two off the hook. So, why don't we just ride it out 'til he's finished? I mean – he has to get this out of his system tonight – and then ask him about Flynn – and the other houses. I mean, we need to get squarely on his side first."

"Damn you, Lines! – O.K."

Soon Peter came up with us, and showed us the stick he was carrying. It was not the four foot, of course. But not a Corporal's cane either. It was the thirty-nine inch willow, about half an inch thick. I said:

"Oh! That's a surprise, I must say. So just three with a Corporal's cane isn't enough. Correct?"

"Quite right!"

When we reached the bathroom Sutton was not there, and Peter said: -

"So let's start with you two. Each one witnesses the other, and the last witnesses Sutton."

So Ian and I went together and I took the first three. It was at least as effective as Collinson's six had been. Then I watched Ian. Peter was honestly doing his best. We were having a good handshake when Sutton came with a paper bag containing about eight packets of twenty Players.
Sutton put them down and said:

"What are you all shaking hands for?"

Ian said:

"Stirzaker was helping us understand that we should have reported you before."

"Oh! I'm sorry, I really will have to give it up."

I couldn't resist saying:

"And you can write us all "thank you" letters on the anniversary date." However, none of us felt like laughing, and Sutton was shaking already. – But smokers often shake.

Sutton didn't do too well, and squeaked a bit. But it must have helped him make up his mind. We all escorted him down to Hall, and watched him toss the whole bag unceremoniously into the kitchen rubbish bin. Then we watched him walk away towards his study before we three walked slowly some distance behind.

Ian started to bring up some of the points we had been talking about, and I could not keep a straight face, even while we were both still in pain. But Peter had been so serious just ten minutes before and now it was all over. The sense of anticlimax hit us all. I think I defused it. Peter surprised us all by saying:

"Do you know, I was thinking just the same on the way up there, and by the time you were both in the bathroom I was on the point of dropping the idea altogether. Then I thought – No! I may as well have some practice before beating Sutton. I knew you two wouldn't really mind anyway." He was genuinely amused at this. Ian didn't see the joke. I think he really did mind.

"Damn you Lines – for the second time tonight!" He

said.

I said:

"Forgive me for being facetious Stirzaker, but perhaps we should all go into East houseroom. Prep has just started, - and you can say to Trace – he's taking prep. 'These people are Tait and Lines. We've just been in the bathroom, and settled a few issues quite firmly. And don't worry – we won't forget it, will we! – No! Really. Your three with that three foot are at least as good as Collinson's six with a Corporal's cane. Hurts like Hell now, in fact'."

Peter said slowly:

"That was facetious, Lines, I might forgive you. You can ask me tomorrow and I'm glad it still hurts. It was meant to."

O dear! My tongue again!

Then we all turned serious as we started to pass the houserooms, and didn't want to be heard laughing as we did so. Peter remarked that so far only Two and Three South was clear of smoke, and half of East House. So he declared his intention to search East number two study immediately and call the House Captains from the other four houses to a meeting before prep was over. Ian went with him to number two to find Sutton coming out. But Sutton had not been quick enough and Flynn's store was discovered. Ian escorted Flynn to the bathroom. As they left, I turned to Peter saying:
-

"May I take a suggestion?"

"What is it?"

"Just that I'm sure you're going to uncover a whole lot

of smoking materials, and you may have some difficulty distinguishing the guilty from the innocent, and still more in finding out who has been protecting whom. So just like the whistling event last term, it might be simpler to leave Ian Tait and me as the only examples of what you think of our behavior. I believe the rest should get the message. I mean you're obviously right to deal with your own house properly – Anyway, if you go after every house the same way, not many house prefects will escape. I hope that speaks for Ian as well. You're going to have a busy night as it is."

"I believe you're right. Except that – if you two are meant to be examples – was three enough? I'll have to think about that; may see you two again later."

Clearly, I could have kept my mouth shut then also. Tait would have been fairly shouting at me:

"Damn you again Lines."

But he did not hear it. I took care not to tell him 'til Peter had closed the whole issue.

So, immediately following the short meeting with the remaining four House Captains there were searches in the eight studies concerned and a further five house prefects were treated the same way as our Sutton and Flynn had been.

Later in the evening there was a knock on our study door.

"Come," said Ian.

Peter Stirzaker came in and we both stood. I closed the door behind him.
"Lines, about your suggestion, (I felt scared at once, still hurting and waiting for him to tell us we were going to have

another three), I'm sure you heard all the activity, and we've been using One North bathroom. Obviously there has been plenty of covering up. And it would be too difficult to find out the whole truth. So the state of affairs now is that they all know how I treated you two, and they also all know that in the future failure to report smoking will be treated just the same as the offence itself. Plenty of frightened people, and probably some guilty as hell and didn't say so. But we'll leave it there, and I think that should be curative. And you two are just lucky – O.K.?"

He turned to me with a smile.

"Thanks very much," we both said, smiling too of course.

"Yes. You've both been a great help." We all had another handshake – and he took his leave.

As he shut the door Ian turned to me:

"Lucky! My - ! Just three still hurts like hell, doesn't it?"

I had to add:

"It was meant to, I thought it was a good beating."
"Damn you again! Lines." Actually he used his favorite nickname for me, which is quite unprintable.

Altogether, it had been a busy time for Stirzaker. At last, the school and house prefects could make a firm stand against smoking. The whole traumatic incident passed into history, and was well remembered. Also, Peter's reputation was even more strongly established especially when the school found out that Ian and I had not escaped. He did not have occasion to stick anyone else for the remainder of that term – about another month.

The following morning I sought out Peter and apologized to him for my words in the corridor the previous evening. He easily accepted, then asked:

"Do you think I sometimes take myself too seriously?"

"Yes, certainly, but the way you're so open, honest, and earnest makes up for it. It keeps on showing through. Not a fault at all. At the beginning of this term, the Headmaster was telling me to be conscious of my faults. And it was my tongue he was talking about. – Pointed me to the Epistle of James – and sure enough it was my tongue again last night. And I suppose in just the same way you'll take yourself seriously all your life. These character traits are so interesting. I mean just look back at the way you had no hesitation at all about caning Tait and me last night. It was all so predictable – exactly what we should have expected. I don't know why we were so surprised. That's what really started me laughing. You were so perfectly in character. I hope you stay that way."

We continued to sit together for English and at the Head's Divinity. As I had been expecting, one day Loveday raised his bushy eyebrows at me and said: -

"The tongue...Lines. The tongue...?"

"Can no man tame," I was sitting opposite Peter on this day and looking at him. "It is an unruly evil, full of deadly poison. Therewith bless we God, even the Father, and therewith curse we men, who are made after the similitude of God. Out of the same mouth proceedeth blessing and cursing. My brethren, these things ought not so to be."

The Head saw that I was smiling a little at Peter as I said this and said to Peter, who had been nodding affirmatively as

I was speaking:

"He has the words perfectly. But is his tongue really tamed yet?"

His insight was uncanny.

Stirzaker had to start to shake his head the other way.

"Alas, not quite yet Sir, but he is improving."

I felt my face turning red. There was about a full minute of silent suspense before the Headmaster continued teaching. Everybody, we agreed afterwards, had felt the tension. After the class, I heard him approach me from behind, and say gently:

"Lines, as usual your mind is able to meet a challenge. Perhaps your prayer-life needs more attention. But well done, so far at least!"

"Thank you Sir!" I felt a wonderful relief.

Loveday was absolute despotes in the school at large, feared, of course, and respected for his great learning and incisive intellect. He seemed to understand his boys better than we did ourselves. His attitude to me seemed ambivalent, realizing that my early scientific bent included distaste for the classical scholarship he espoused.

I became able to reconcile the complexities, understanding what Mark had meant by using me to serve a wider purpose. It was deeply humiliating, yet balanced by Mark's evident respect for me, crowned by his confession:

"Thank God it's you" – coming just two weeks after having caned me soundly. So he, in turn, was resolving his own problems and acknowledging my help.

Yet Loveday accepted me, unbaptized, under his care. Perhaps he held to the hope that I might mature enough to enter the Anglican pathway or even entertain a call to the Priesthood. Three years after leaving school I had a charming long hand letter from him, with warm congratulations on my Tripos results. I should have replied, and told him that I had finally made a decision to profess Christian faith. He would have rejoiced to hear of this answer to his prayer.

My Mother had never understood him. She related my parents' visit to the school in '39, when she had been struck by his failure to react to her feminine beauty, as she had come to expect any man to do. When they reached the S.E. entrance to the Speech Hall, where many boys were writing exams, he had turned to her, solemnly saying: "Allow me" and removed a cigarette from her mouth as she took a puff. Of course, the fault had been hers to have been so rude as to smoke in his presence. His monasticism grated upon her.

One day, in class (I forget whether Divinity or Latin) when he happened to have brought a cane with him, he remarked: "Scientists are always happy when they know the formula".

Then, pointing his stick in my direction, said:

"Spell that word, Lines."

I did so, slowly, longing to add an "r" to the end, but much too frightened to do so. I could have pointed out that in a maths or physics exam there was often a requirement. "Prove any formula you use".

Stirzaker had been congratulated by the Head and several others for his determined actions to root out smoking from the whole of the prefecture. And Ian Tait and I were both agreeably surprised when no one made any comments while we were exposed at the regular Wednesday East House swim nights. Flynn and Sutton were more vivid, and obviously, Peter's three foot was more effective than a Corporal's cane, but not nearly as damaging as Mark's four foot. They had no scar at all. All these comparisons and contrasts were freely discussed by the boys. The important consensus was that smoking was a habit to avoid.

By about half-term or a little after, the V-1 menace came under better control. Launching sites were discovered and destroyed by aircraft attacks. But more importantly the anti-aircraft defense line was moved from its previous position South of the Capital to the Kent and East Sussex coast, so that increasing numbers of incoming flying bombs failed to reach land before being shot down.

However, the Hun came up with a new weapon, the V-2. This was a ballistic missile, guided during the first, rocket-propelled part of its flight, so that its parabolic path would lead to a landing somewhere in the Greater London area. The accuracy of this weapon was remarkable, in that few of them strayed into the surrounding counties, as so many V-1's had done. The first inkling we had at school was that sometimes there was a loud explosion heard without any preceding motor-bike exhaust popping sound. Later we realized that the explosions were heard in pairs.

Peter and I contrived to sit near the back of the Speech Hall during Higher Certificate Exams, and often we would raise two fingers at each other as we identified these double-bangs. It was not until after the war that the cause of these was explained. The incoming missile was descending almost vertically at a high supersonic speed. There was no sound warning of its imminent arrival, so that sheltering from it was impossible. In addition, after the missile had exploded the sound emitted by the oblique shock from the pointed nose would be heard as the second bang.

The weather was good for the heats and finals of athletics. Jake was organizing these details. Peter easily won the hundred and the furlong. Ian Tait attained the final of one of the middle distances. I was excluded after the first heats of the quarter and the one-mile. The House had difficulty raising a four-by-four-forty relay team, and I had to do one of the legs. I was pounding round the last bend as hard as I could, which was not very fast at all, when I noticed Blackshaw standing, quite by himself just inside the tracks. As I passed, he said:

"You're not running Lines."

No one else was near enough to hear this. But I was going as fast as I could (Who wouldn't). Charles B. Blackshaw was popular as a housemaster and on Christian name terms with some of his house, including Ian Tait, who had earned his colours for inter-house fives when only fifteen. Tait was always nimble on his feet, and a good batter. C.B.B. well knew that I cared little for rugger and had a poor eye for a ball. He must have seen that I regarded cricket as a waste of time. But when he saw his House relay team doing badly, he could have tried encouragement. This remark was clearly for me alone to hear, and left me disappointed in him. I had always imagined him leading his platoon across no-man's land on the Somme, but he had shown himself in a different light.

In fact the events at the end of Lent term had led me to be confident that in war and under fire I could follow his example and not crack, but be cool, firm, decisive and always in the lead, as he had been. So I had had a loosely affectionate respect for him. But he spoiled that with a few words.

Oddly, I failed to forgive him. Of course I ought to have cleared it with him soon afterward. I had so easily forgiven Mark for the pain that I could never forget, the after-pains that kept coming back, even after I had left the school and for the scars that are still there, also Dennis and Peter likewise for their parts in this story, and of course that wonderful man of many talents, Beaumont. Life was too short to entertain any hurt. But I suffered some regret on hearing years later that Charles had died of a brain tumor.

11 EPILOGUE

It has been difficult to trace most of my friends. Of those mentioned, Bull was killed during aircrew training. Calvert's bomber burned up at the end of a runway. Trace did well in the Navy. Capt A.C. Wray, R.N. joined the Coast Guard after his retirement. Ian Tait spent three years in the Navy, and was minesweeping until well after the war. He later entered General Practice after qualifying from Bart's two years ahead of me. Peter Stirzaker moved to Australia as a consulting engineer. Two of our choristers were music scholars at King's College, Cambridge when I was in John's choir under Herbert Howells. Sutton stayed at school at least one term longer, won a scholarship in Modern Languages to Selwyn College Cambridge and later took Holy Orders. John Mark became a first class athlete, and had the honour of carrying the Olympic flame round White City Stadium in 1948 –must have been unforgettable – six foot two inches, fair haired, aquiline with a long, easy stride, and moving very fast. Ironically, I was the only other person from that clutch to attain proximity to the '48 Olympics, when we reached the final of the Senior Eight Championship in Ireland – used as the last step of the elimination for the Irish Eight.

I had not been aware of Mark's achievements – he had represented Gr. Britain in the 400 metres – until I saw the historic picture in a daily paper of him on the track at Wembley. I should have congratulated him then. He would have been delighted to hear that I, having earned a few scars four years before, had done well in any sport, after having not attained any distinction at school. But he was immersed in clinical medicine study and I was serving an engineering apprenticeship in Belfast. The opportunity passed and now he is dead.

Old Cranleighans fought well, with a roll of Honour numbering one hundred and fifty, equivalent to three years of total school intake. Sad! But dulce et decorum est. I was in good company. Life has been wonderful so far and I may have served God, yet cannot escape some regret for having never served my Country actively in time of war.